ADVANCE PRAISE

"Worth its weight in gold! Whether you are a beginning negotiator or a seasoned one, this book provides specific tools and real world examples so that you can avoid critical mistakes, and ensure a winning outcome. It is a powerful guidebook for negotiating in any scenario and in any industry."

~*Robert Shapiro, Esq., Renowned Trial Lawyer, Co-Founder of Legal Zoom and RightCounsel.com*

"Navigating difficult personalities is hard, but negotiating with them can feel impossible. Rebecca's book will show readers methods to get what they want, even when negotiating in extraordinarily challenging circumstances."

~*Laura Wasser, Esq., Celebrity Divorce Attorney and Founder of It's Over Easy*

"As a fierce divorce attorney, Rebecca Zung knows how to negotiate even under the toughest of conditions. But even if you're not experiencing divorce, learning how to negotiate from a position of strength and inner confidence will help you in

i

your career, no matter what area you're in. This book provides real guidance on getting you from where you are now to where you want to be."

~ Tamsen Fadal, Emmy Award Winning Television Journalist, News Anchor and Bestselling Author

"Rebecca Zung's book – Negotiate Like You M.A.T.T.E.R. – is the answer to a prayer – especially for those of us who fall into being too nice or too accommodating to others when it comes to asking for what we truly want and deserve. This book came to me in perfect timing to negotiate an important legal settlement, and I'll be forever grateful. This is the perfect resource for when you feel you are dealing with a narcissist or someone who is more powerful. You'll learn exactly how to get those types of personalities to give you what you want, or something even better."

~Nancy Juetten, Thought Leader and Bestselling Author of the Bye-Bye Boring Bio Workbook

Negotiate Like YOU M.A.T.T.E.R.

The Sure-Fire Method to Step Up and Win

By Rebecca Zung, Esq.

Foreword by Robert Shapiro

NEGOTIATE LIKE YOU M.A.T.T.E.R.: THE SURE FIRE METHOD TO STEP UP AND WIN

For anyone who wants to get what they want

Contents

FOREWORD

Not long ago, U.S. Supreme Court Justice Ruth Bader Ginsberg was honored by her alma mater, Columbia Law School, on the 25th anniversary of her appointment to the highest court in the land. In her acceptance speech, she posed a challenge to the students in attendance. She exhorted them to refrain from falling prey to the lure of the almighty "hourly rate." "If you are a true professional," Justice Ginsberg shared, "you will use your degree to make things a little better for other people."

This year, I celebrated 50 years as a member of the California Bar, and I am proud that I have dedicated my career to being not just a lawyer, but also a counselor in the truest sense of the word. As attorneys and counselors-at-law, we are mandated to be public servants. By providing our knowledge, skills and wisdom to others, we empower and propel others into better lives, and then those that we have empowered can turn around and lend a hand to someone else. Through Legal Zoom and RightCounsel.com, I have devoted much of my time, energy and career to making otherwise inaccessible information, accessible. Those entities put power into the hands of every day citizens.

I normally am not a fan of divorce attorneys and their positions. It has been my experience that they often over-litigate, causing further and unnecessary discord among families. This discord is often irreparable. I believe that family law cases should be mediated and resolved in a manner that allows for couples and their children to heal, so that they can move forward with the skills they will so desperately need for healthy communication in their newly created futures.

It is precisely for that reason, that I was drawn to Rebecca Zung and her work. She and I have a shared vision to use our positions as lawyers to expand our reach to those who cannot necessarily afford to hire good counsel. Through her media appearances, books, podcast and speaking engagements, she is a conduit for people to gain access to knowledge, methods and strategies, all of which transforms lives.

"Negotiation Like You M.A.T.T.E.R." goes right to the heart of what we all need. We all want to know that we are valued. We all want to feel seen, heard and understood. Many people often find themselves in the misguided place of hustling for that feeling that they matter by engaging in tactics that in the long run, cost thousands of unnecessary dollars, and even more grave, steal their souls. The litigation path is often the cowardly one. Many choose to use the justice system as a sword because they find that path more palatable and less onerous than actually having to have a real conversation.

Until now, a productive dialogue toward the goal of resolution has been lacking because we haven't put the right tools in people's hands. This book delivers the complete gamut of information, giving readers exactly the areas upon which to concentrate, from the internal to the external, so that both sides' need to feel valued is satisfied. The information provided here is worth its weight in gold. Whether you are a beginning negotiator or a seasoned one, this book provides specific tools and real world examples so that you can avoid critical mistakes, and ensure a winning outcome. It is a powerful guidebook for negotiating in any scenario and in any industry.

The world in which we currently live is in turmoil. Our nation is deeply polarized, politically, racially and spiritually. Recent events have shined a spotlight on the rampancy of ongoing misogyny. The divorce rate remains high. We are in crisis, and our ability to communicate with each other is seriously diseased. This is an epidemic. The antidote is not more hate, but rather learning to communicate powerfully.

Abraham Lincoln was able to unite this country at a time when it was at its most deeply divided. He wisely stated, "Do I not destroy my enemies when I make them my friends?"

It is my sincerest hope that the readers of this book implement the methodology in this book into their lives, igniting a worldwide movement toward dynamic discussions that promote peaceful agreements. I look forward to the day when we destroy all our enemies by making them our friends.

~Robert Shapiro, Esq.
Renowned Trial Lawyer, Co-Founder of Legal Zoom and RightCounsel.com

PREFACE

This book began as a presentation. Many years ago, while I was still in the growth phase of my law practice, I realized that if I wanted to give talks to local associations and groups, I would have to come up with something to talk about other than divorce. Because while more than 50% of first marriages end in divorce (the statistics are worse for subsequent marriages), no one really wanted to hear me talk about divorce. So I came up with three different presentations which I could offer to local rotary clubs, professional organizations, women's groups, and so forth, so they would invite me to come and speak. One of the presentations I crafted was a talk I called "High Powered Negotiation Skills". If I were asked to speak to a women's group, then it became "High Powered Negotiation Skills for Women".

The talk served me well and helped me grow my practice. At no time, did I ever consider it to be another book or anything more than the presentation. As the years went by, the talk became more and more popular and in the past year, I have been asked to present it as the Keynote Speaker for the American Bar Association's Mediation Section, as a presenter to the national women's networking organization, Ellevate, and to former Today Show producer, Tammi Leader Fuller's brainchild for empowering women, Campowerment.

I have been speaking for years. As a teacher and a litigation courtroom attorney, being nervous was something *other* people experienced. Until I was the Keynote at the American Bar Association. That was the first place I felt a butterfly (or two) because these were my peers, professionals who negotiated all day, every day. What was I going to teach them about negotiation? Imagine my surprise when I received notes from the older, white guy lawyers, who had been practicing for years, about how moved they were, and how much their practices were positively impacted by my talk.

Then when I presented for Ellevate, I had more than 400 women on the webinar and I couldn't physically keep up with the avalanche of questions. I was astounded. These were businesswomen who were certainly successful in their own right. But they were searching for ways to get better at achieving their next level of performance.

At Campowerment, one of the women who came to hear my presentation was a soon-to-be divorcee, with two teenagers at home. She was looking for advice on how to handle her upcoming divorce negotiations. We chatted for a few moments directly after hearing me speak, but we continued our dialogue through email after Campowerment had ended. Then out of the blue, I received a note from her. She had been so inspired by my story of going to law school at night with three little children at home as a single, newly divorced mom, that she had made the decision to go back to medical school! I was astounded. She will be 54 years old when she finishes medical school. I often think of the Dear Abby response when a reader asked her if she should go back to medical school – she said "How old will you be in 4 years if you don't go to medical school?" She had learned to get what she wanted, just by listening to my presentation and implementing what she had learned.

It was through realizing the profound impact that learning "the how" of negotiation can have on people that made me realize I had to write this book, create resources and dedicate my life to giving people the tools they need to annihilate inhibitions, step up and win.

I have a lot of people to thank for getting this book into physical form.

Thank you to the universe, for being present and ready to respond with what I want at all times.

Thank you to my husband John, my best friend and partner in this life journey for 21 years and counting. Thanks for picking me up in law school when we were kids! I can't believe the life we have created and wouldn't want to do this human thing with anyone else.

Thank you to my children, Alexander, Nicholas, Danielle and Emma. And to their chosen spouses who I now call my daughters and son – in –"love" because I love them too, Natalie,

Sara and Freddy. To my grandchildren, who are just pure joy and pure love, Trey, Catalina and Joseph. You are all my reason. Period.

Thank you also:

To my parents, Max M.-K. Zung, MD and Madeline Roye Zung, for believing in me, loving me and giving me a kickass gene pool.

To my brother, Michael Zung, for being my first best friend and my partner in crime for all of your life and nearly all of mine.

To Caroline Cederquist, for being the best of the best friends that anyone could have.

To Kelly Townsend – gratitude for you always.

To my dear cousin, Ken Ross, and my friend, Nancy Juetten, for being invaluable sounding boards and for your great ideas for this book.

To Erica Glessing, for helping me to make my visions a reality in the world.

To Robert Shapiro for offering to write the foreword for this book. I am beyond honored and eternally grateful. Your participation guarantees that many more people will get access to this information – meaning many more lives will be transformed.

To all of my dearest family and friends who constantly believe in me, support me, make me laugh, and just make my life better every day. I am so grateful the universe put me in your space and vice versa.

To all who read this book, I am grateful for the opportunity to use what I have learned to help make your journey a little easier.

Namaste,
Rebecca Zung, Esq.

Introduction

*"Everything is negotiable. Whether or not the negotiation
is easy is another thing."*
~*Carrie Fisher*

Sweaty palms. Heart racing. Fear. Can't breathe. Is it a horror film? Close. It's just you trying to negotiate. For the majority of us, asking for what we want in general can be difficult, but just the thought of negotiating can be debilitating. But here's the paradox. We are negotiating all day long, every day, professionally and personally. Do you want more vacation time? More pay? To sell more of your product or services at price commensurate with your value? A seat on an influential committee? A bank loan? How about a better marriage or personal relationship? Or to get your teenager to clean his or her room? When most of us think of negotiating, we think of buying a car or a house. The other type of negotiating we think of is for something in our careers. We don't usually think of it in terms of our personal lives, but the truth is we often don't even realize when we've walked into a negotiation situation.

Negotiation skills are one of those sets of life skills, like finance, which everyone needs, and no one gets formal training for, probably no matter what your "formal" training is. They don't even teach negotiation skills in law school, where you'd think they would.

I cut my teeth and really learned the art of negotiation as a divorce attorney where I litigated (and continue to litigate) complex, high net worth, very emotional cases. I always say there is a divorce paradox, and that is that during one of the most traumatic times of your life, (and divorce and death are always at the top of every list of the most traumatic things we could ever possibly experience) you have to make the most critical decisions of your life. So while you're experiencing abject fear, burning resentment, potentially deep fury, heartbreaking sadness and grief, you have to somehow belly up to the negotiation table, bring all your senses to bear, and think clearly because the future of all the things that mean the most to you teeters in the balance. Your children. Your money. Your home. Your business. The things you hold most dear require that you negotiate with the finesse of Warren Buffett closing a deal. How the heck are you supposed to do that?

For most of us, simply asking for what we want can be a challenge. Even in our most intimate relationships, communicating what you want, your preferences, your desires, can be a complex undertaking. Why is it that the more you have at stake, the harder negotiating can be? Sometimes just the thought of it can cause that shortness of breath and panicked feeling. We often cringe when asking for something – anything for ourselves and can feel embarrassment, guilt, shame or fear.

So then what often happens is we just don't say anything. We don't like conflict, so we end up agreeing to things we don't want or that we end up regretting. Our fight or flight takes over, and flight ends up winning. While that protective cover may feel safe and that it is the best thing to do at that time, as the feeling of safety sets in, and then eventually wears off, another more insidious feeling starts to creep in – which is way worse. That is resentment. Resentment that you settled for less than you would have, and resentment that the other person "got away" with more than he or she should have. Resentment is one of the most toxic emotions a human can experience. It ruins perfectly good relationships and eats you alive from the inside out.

The statistics for negotiating are fairly dismal. According to a recent Robert Half survey, only 39% of employees tried to negotiate pay with their last job offer. Of that 39%, 46% were males and 35% were females. Another survey reveals that only 7% of women and 57% of men have *ever* negotiated their salaries.

And guess what? If you think it's any easier for women lawyers – you know the ones allegedly who are trained to argue and win – think again. According to a study published by the

American Bar Association, (and performed by the U.S. Census Bureau) in 2014, the median pay for full-time female lawyers was 77.4 percent of the pay earned by their male counterparts. In all law-related jobs, median pay for female workers in 2014 was 51.6 percent of the pay received by male workers. It gets worse the higher up women lawyers go. The difference in average compensation for male and female partners at top U.S. law firms amounts to a 53 percent pay gap. Interestingly enough, the gap was only 44% a few years back. Yes, you read that correctly. It's actually getting worse for female lawyers, not better.

Incredulously, the legal profession overall has a wide gender pay gap, but sadly, other fields are not immune. Overall, when there are no controls over the pay in an industry, females make $.78 on every male dollar. Even in female-dominated industries such as nursing and teaching, men make more. In male dominated industries, such as financial advising or software development, the gap grows even wider.

Why is this? Women are afraid of looking difficult or being perceived as difficult. This is with good reason. A fascinating study/experiment was performed several years ago at Columbia Business School. The business students there were divided into two groups, both men and women in each half of the class. All students in both groups were then given a story to read. The story was identical. The story was a rags to riches inspirational one where the protagonist came up through the ranks to become a very successful venture capitalist.

Then the students were asked questions about the likeability of the protagonist. And guess what? That's right. Howard was likeable, a hero, to be revered. They'd love him as a boss, a mentor, or on their team. Heidi? Not so much. She was to be respected. Absolutely. But in short, she was a difficult person who they didn't really think was likeable and certainly not one they wanted as a boss or on their team. Same exact story other than the gender of the protagonist. What a difference pronouns can make. The moral of the Howard/Heidi story is that there is a reason why women shrink from asserting themselves. It's not just women though.

Men are not immune. While it's not discussed as often, men are often afraid to assert themselves too. They have all the same concerns. They fear that rejection. Their fear may come from a different place but all of us spend a huge chunk of our day trying to make ourselves look as good as possible, or maybe even more so, avoiding trying to look bad.

So while not all of you will go through a divorce, or end up negotiating for the release of hostages, you will end up negotiating to try to get something you want, something that is very important to you. The skills I have honed in my more than 20 years as one of the Top 1% of attorneys in the country will translate to you, in your life and in your town, no matter what you do for a living, or what your situation is. I've represented the most affluent business people in the most complex financial situations, and parents who are in the fight of their lives over their children. The bottom line is that by guiding people through the worst survival negotiations of their lives, I have realized that certain skills have emerged as being the absolute necessities for getting what you want in any aspect of your life.

There is a way to get what you want, and feel good about it (yes, that's right – no guilt). Even better, there is a way not only to get what you want, but also have the other side feel good about your getting what you want also. Yes, it is possible! This book will walk you through the methodology to get there.

Chapter 1 – We All Want to Matter

"People just want to know they matter."
~ Oprah Winfrey

I t was 9 PM in the evening. I was sitting in another divorce attorney's small conference room, in the same chair in which I had been sitting for now a full 12 hours, when the mediator burst into the room and asked to speak with me privately, away from my client. The table, which allegedly was glass, had been completely covered with papers and documents related to a large, somewhat complicated divorce, which had accumulated throughout an arduous day of negotiation. The new "tablecloth" included ten versions of an asset and liability distribution schedule, marked up bank statements, old tax returns, notes that had been passed, and on top of all that, a smattering of empty coffee cups, granola bar wrappers, pens, highlighters and calculators.

My client, I'll call him Randy, was a very powerful businessman. A towering presence at 6'5", he ran one of the largest development companies in Florida at the time. He had been responsible for developing large residential communities throughout the state. He prided himself on being steely, savvy and a bit ruthless in his business deals. In fact, in his initial meeting with me, while sitting in my law offices, just before executing the engagement agreement, he looked at me and said, "Any wiggle room in your retainer amount or your hourly fee?" I had the top practice in that area at the time and had plenty of business, so it was very easy for me to respond, "Nope!" and then I added, "and you wouldn't respect me if I did." He faked a weak laugh, and then retained me.

The day of mediation, we had been trying to resolve the entire divorce case with a neutral mediator, with whom I had worked before on thousands of cases. This was an 18-year marriage – long term by most people's standards in general, but also, and more importantly for this particular case, by Florida law's standards. Anything over 17 years is considered long term, and the prize or penalty (depending upon which side of the fence you are on) is permanent alimony (which means it lasts until one of the parties dies or the party cashing those monthly alimony checks, remarries). A life sentence – or a grand prize – and obviously a very hotly contested issue in nearly all cases where this is a possibility. Of course, other factors are considered, such as the ages of the parties, the disparity in incomes, the health of the parties and other considerations. In Randy's case, however, he was definitely looking down what he considered to be both barrels of the alimony life sentence gun.

"Lidia", Randy's soon to be ex-wife, was sitting in another conference room, a much larger and grander version of the one we'd been looking at all day, because we had all agreed weeks before to mediate at her lawyer's office. While the parties had no children, Lidia had not worked during the marriage. A slight woman, she was deep into middle age, her face slightly lined and her dyed hair stubbornly still showed some gray. To say that she was downtrodden would have been a stretch, but she did come across as resigned. Resigned that her marriage was over, resigned that her life hadn't quite gone as planned. Her lawyer, a woman I had known for several years at that point, explained to me that her client was a bit emotional about the breakup and resolution would be more likely if we mediated at her offices. After some discussion with my client, he agreed.

The mediator, Chris, was also a lawyer, but had dedicated his career to mediating. He had worked hard throughout the day to get us to a place where we actually had worked through the majority of the issues. By the time he burst through the doors and asked to speak to me privately, his tie and jacket had long been thrown on a chair, and we were either expecting a draft of the marital settlement agreement to review or the pronouncement that the other side was done negotiating.

With a measured look of confoundment on his face, Chris asked me to step outside the conference room to speak to him.

As I walked out of the room, I looked back at my client, who had an equally puzzled expression, and told him I would be right back. Out in the now dark reception area (the receptionist had left hours before), Chris said, "I have a highly unusual offer from the wife." I steeled myself, because those words, at that time of the day, usually meant we were probably about done. The next stop after a failed mediation in divorce? A full-blown trial. My mind raced. Now I was going to have to set the case for trial, and did I have time to handle another trial, and would the client even want to pay the fees and costs for a major trial? But he would have no choice. Back to reality.

"What kind of unusual offer?" I asked cautiously.

"In my 30 years of practicing law, and 20 years of mediating divorce cases, I haven't ever seen this before," he starts.

"Okay. What is it?" I ask again, my curiosity now thoroughly piqued and starting to blur into annoyance.

"She is willing to waive permanent alimony completely if…" and he looks at me and laughs just slightly…

"Yes?" I say, now actually annoyed.

"He apologizes to her for everything he did that caused the marriage to fail," Chris finally spits out.

Now I am taken aback. At that point, I had handled thousands of divorces. I had certainly heard my share of people who wanted people to feel remorse, to do penance, to suffer, to pay and on and on. But an apology in exchange for a *waiver of permanent alimony*??

Unheard of.

To put it into perspective, he was going to be paying her $15,000 per month in alimony or $180,000 per year. Both parties were 53 years old. In Florida, the payor party can apply for a modification of permanent alimony after the age of 65 and only if his or her income has actually been reduced as a result of retiring. If the payor's income remained level due to passive income from assets, pension or other sources, then no modification would be warranted. But let's assume he would have retired at the age of 65, he still would have paid her $180,000 for 12 years.

The total? Over $2 Million Dollars!!

So back into the cubby hole conference room, where my client awaited with bated breath, I proceeded to share the unusual offer with him, thinking, apparently erroneously, that he would jump at that chance.

Nope. Wrong.

"Why would I do that?" he exclaimed upon hearing the offer.

"Because it would save you millions of dollars in permanent alimony," I replied, stating the obvious.

"I'm not doing that," he said resolutely, crossing his arms and staring at my disbelieving eyes.

I blinked and then I took a deep breath, and said calmly and deliberately, "If she just wants you to go over there, sit in the room with her alone for five minutes, give her a heartfelt apology, and in exchange, you're off the hook for permanent

11

alimony, then that's what you're going to do. Millions of monied spouses around the country would kill to be in this position right now. So swallow your pride, get up, walk over there and apologize!"

With the reluctance of a teenager being forced to do chores, he slowly arose and with his head down, and shuffled out of the room with the mediator.

Several minutes later he returned, a much brighter look on his face. The mediator, then returned a few minutes after speaking with the wife and reported that we finally, after now 13 hours of mediating, had a deal. They would equally divide the assets and she would waive permanent alimony.

To the naked eye, this whole exchange seems incredulous on multiple levels. Who in their right mind would give up $2 million dollars just to get an apology?? And then what crazy person would choose losing $2 million instead of apologizing?

The answer laid deep within the recesses of those two human beings. The answer is the highlight, the centerpiece of what's happening in not just that negotiation, but in every negotiation.

So what was really going on in that scenario?

Do I Matter?

When Oprah gave up her regular daytime talk show after having done it for several years, she said that what she had learned after doing thousands of interviews – interviews with heads of state, major power celebrities, drug addicts, stay at home mothers, elderly people, children, and people from every walk of life – that there is a common denominator in the human experience that we all share:

"We all want to know that what we do, what we say and who we are, matters. We want to be validated. Every single person, in every single confrontation, every single encounter that you have, whether it's with the guy in the supermarket, or at the toll booth, or your boss or your children, every argument is really about do you see me? Do you <u>see</u> me? Does what I say mean anything to you? **Do I matter to you?"**

When I heard her say that, it started me thinking about what's going on in relationships and divorce negotiations, but then quickly I realized that this thought, this principle, this truism, is really at the heart of every negotiation. I've been an attorney for a long time, and divorce law is the only kind of law I've ever practiced. So while I don't have any formal training as a psychologist (I did get my life coaching certification), I have had to be not only a lawyer, but a therapist, life coach and cheerleader for my clients. I have been at the front lines of the most powerful negotiations there are. What means more or is more personal to people than their children, their money, their homes, or their businesses?

After hearing Oprah's words, I realized that at the heart of every negotiation, is exactly what she said. The truth is that you can be the most skilled negotiation specialist there is, and if you miss the basic underlying principle that every human being wants to feel as if they matter, then you will not get what you want.

In looking at my opening story, which is a true story by the way, what was really happening there? From the wife's perspective, she probably had never felt validated by the husband and had never felt that she had mattered much to him. She also probably knew that an apology from him was a big deal. We didn't ever discuss whether or not he had ever apologized to her before, but more than likely, he hadn't. He had a personality that in the current world, might be characterized as narcissistic. Whether he actually would have been diagnosed as a narcissist in the clinical sense, really was of no import to the wife in this case. She just knew what her experience had been in interacting with him.

Randy was a guy who wasn't going to easily admit that he was wrong. He was used to people doing what he wanted, when he wanted, and he also basically did what he wanted. He was wealthy and powerful, a combination that doesn't usually come with the humility trait. While both parties contribute to the breakdown of the marriage, and thus, I am certain she was not perfect, it was clear from that interaction that took place right then, that after 18 years of marriage and seemingly the same number of hours in mediation, she just desperately wanted to know that she had mattered to him.

Why didn't the husband want to apologize initially? Even in the face of saving millions of dollars in alimony payments? Going back to the basic premise that all humans want to know that they matter, the way that he felt that he mattered and had value in the world, was through his tough exterior. Using the façade of being powerful, rich and in control, he felt valuable in the world. Paying alimony, as painful as that would have been, and it was definitely something he didn't want to do, in a twisted way, played into his value proposition. If he paid her alimony, then she would need him, he would still have control over her, he would get to tell the world that he makes so much money that he had to pay her alimony and the list goes on. But an apology? That didn't work within his self-built web of external value at all. While he understood on an intellectual level that it meant saving millions of dollars, on an emotional level, that meant peeling off some of those layers of control, which while on a level that certainly was subconscious, meant that he, in a sense, was actually de-valuing himself. In short, he felt he would matter less if he apologized to her.

The Added Layer

While this sort of dynamic goes on all the time between human beings when they are interacting normally with each other, in a negotiation there is an added layer. That added layer is that not only are both humans vying to be seen, to know that they matter, to feel that they have value and are respected and appreciated, but there is also a formal transaction involved. At that end of this interaction, there will be a formal agreement, an exchange of promises or services, and more than likely, a writing or some form of memorializing the conversation. This is what distinguishes negotiation from any other type of human interaction. In other words, the measurement of our "worth" is going to be in the outcome of the negotiation. It may sound dramatic, but it is true. That is why we hate to negotiate. We don't want to feel as though we are less somehow because we didn't get out of the negotiation what we thought we should.

If you haven't done your internal growth work, then what will happen is that at the deepest, darkest level, a "loss" in negotiations will feel as though we ARE less, not just that we RECEIVED less.

The combination of higher stakes in the negotiation conversation, along with the human experience of feeling the innate, instinctive and almost carnal need to protect that baby inner self that needs to know that he or she matters, can feel deadly to most people. That's why most people don't bother to do it. Statistics show that on average only about 29% of people have ever negotiated their salaries, yet those same statistics show that 84% of the people who ask for more money in their jobs will get it. With those figures, one might scratch their head and wonder why more people wouldn't ask for more money.

The answer is at once, very simple and also very complicated. The biggest fears people list when asked about why they don't negotiate are:

1. Fear of rejection
2. Fear of looking bad (too aggressive, too needy, too demanding, and so forth)
3. Fear of not knowing what to say or do
4. Fear of conflict
5. Fear of the unknown
6. Fear of not having enough information
7. Fear of losing the deal/job/offer
8. Fear of looking incompetent
9. Fear of not being valued for your knowledge
10. Fear of seeming inappropriate

A review of all of the above reveals that they all tie back to my core idea of what's happening in a negotiation, which is:

I know I matter. And I also know you want to know you matter. I want you to see that I matter.

The fear people experience is that of being exposed. We don't want to risk being vulnerable because if we aren't successful in negotiations, then we might feel that we don't matter or aren't valued, thereby exposing our deepest vulnerabilities. That risk is often too much to bear.

I have lectured on negotiation for years. I have delivered the talk to rooms of 20 and to rooms of hundreds. To women's groups, men's groups and mixed company. I have written many articles on negotiation, and have a chapter about it in my first book, *Breaking Free: A Step by Step Divorce Guide to Achieving Emotional, Physical and Spiritual Freedom.* But until recently, my talks and articles were mostly focused on the external skills, the skills that most books, articles and training courses focus on. In my humble opinion, most resources, while helpful, are missing the foundational piece – which bears repeating – **I know I matter. And I also know you want to know you matter. I want you to see that I matter.**

Once I had the "AHA" moment that this is what's really going on at the heart of any negotiation, I went back and did an analysis of my negotiation "steps" to see if this core principle applied to each one of the steps. I even talked it through with my colleagues, friends and family. They cautioned me to not "force" the steps to fit into the message. They said that if they didn't fit, then I would have to address them in my book as a separate step, unrelated to the basic idea. But somewhat unsurprisingly, they all went right back to the core message.

With that in mind I set about to build a methodology that all people could use in all walks of life, and that would work in any negotiation. The bottom line in any negotiation is both people want to get what they want. They both want to walk away feeling like they received value, because if they received value, then that must mean that they are valuable. That they have been seen. That they matter.

The "You M.A.T.T.E.R. Negotiation Method" Was Born

I really wanted a way that anyone who is negotiating can remember the steps, especially while in the midst of a potentially stressful situation. Thus, I have created a way to remember the steps by using the word that means the most to all of us humans – MATTER. I will present the steps to you here, and then each chapter will be dedicated to a letter. They are:

M – My Value is Defined by ME

A – Analyze the Research and Create Arguments and Leverage

Dress to a "**T**" – Then Use Those Power Words and Body Language

T - Tackle the Hard Issues Second (Agreed Issues First)

Keep Your **E**motions in Check

R – Record All Agreements in Writing

All of the above will make a lot more sense in the coming chapters. My approach to negotiation is an "inside out" process. That means you start from your inside and work your way outward. To that end, the methodology in the You M.A.T.T.E.R. Method is this:

1. Work on your inner self – your brain, your emotions, your own feeling of value, worth and knowing that you matter.
2. Do the homework you need to do to do prepare for the conversation; and
3. Negotiate

Not a figure based in actual statistics but one that I like to use is that **80% of winning a negotiation takes place before you even walk into the room.** When looking at the above layers of steps, think of your internal self as being 50% of the work, think of external research and preparation as being 30% of the work and think of the day of negotiation as being 20% of getting you to getting what you want, when you want it and on what terms.

That means the hardest work is going to be done on yourself. That step starts with realizing that we must take responsibility for our own actions and that we create our realities. The flip side of not being able to blame anyone else for where we are in our lives right now, is the exquisite realization that we have total control over our own reality. I once saw Will Smith in an interview express that one just needs to decide what his or her life is going to be, when it's going to happen and how it's going to happen, and the universe will make it so. This is a truism.

The key is to take the steps to drive the outcomes that you want, and this book will give you all the tools you will need to get there.

So, with that, ladies and gentlemen, let's begin!

Chapter 2 – "M" – My Value is Defined By Me

"You either walk inside your story and own it or you stand outside your story and hustle for your worthiness."
~Brené Brown

TAKEAWAYS FROM THIS CHAPTER:

- You and you alone define your personal or *intrinsic* feelings of value.
- You can get rid of old thoughts that aren't serving you and create a new self that feels whole and complete
- You can apply the principles of physics and neuroscience to declare your new self and live from that place.
- By declaring your new self and living in that place with complete integrity, you will establish your baseline of feeling valuable
- Because people think what you tell them to think, you will show tell them to see and know your value, once you have established it for yourself
- Communicating your value is the first step toward getting what you want in a negotiation.

You and You Alone Define Your Value

Value in a negotiation comes in two ways. There is the value that you define using extrinsic measures and then there are your own feelings of internal value. We are all internally valuable. You are born, you are alive, you are unique and you were meant to be here. You have inherent internal value. While you will definitely need to do your homework to establish your position for the external value of something like a job, or a raise, or a promotion or your product, your internal value will remain constant, immoveable. The very first step to a successful negotiation starts right inside your own brain. For anyone else to see your value, to acknowledge that you matter, you will have to demonstrate that. You will have to burst into that room with an absolute knowing that you are whole and complete and that nothing that the other person can say or do can rock that core.

People will think what you tell them to think. And you want to communicate that you are valuable, so that the other side feels that getting something from you is of value. Psychologically, we are wired to want to something we can't have, or that we think is better than what we have now. Your job in a negotiation is communicate to the other person the value they are getting by working with you, extrinsically *and* intrinsically.

Because your intrinsic value is the most important part of the foundation of a successful negotiation, you must start there.

I Am Whole

I haven't always been a skilled negotiator, nor have I always felt as if had value, let alone knew how to define it. I grew up fairly sheltered in an upper middle class neighborhood in McLean, Virginia. My father, who emigrated from China with his family of origin as a teenager, was Chief of Anesthesia at a hospital in Washington D.C., and my mother, who is of German descent, started off in the operating room as a surgical nurse, but then went on to create her own successful real estate company.

Spending time hustling for my worthiness was not just a hobby for me, unfortunately. Like so many others, I was bullied as a child. Bullied for being Chinese, and probably more so because I was vulnerable and bullies, like sharks, smell the blood of vulnerability. I detested being half Chinese, hated that my middle name is Yu-Kang, and always felt different. I distinctly remember being at recess, and while the ringleader of the bullies was hurling her insults, I spoke my silent mantra.

You all are a bunch of losers. I don't need any of you. One day I am going to show all of you that I am smarter than you, prettier than you, and better than you in every way that you can imagine.

It didn't really stop the pain of the bullying at the time. They knew they had a weak one. One that already felt like the oddball, and wasn't sure I fit in. Those years formed the basis of my standing outside of my story and spending the rest of my career as an attorney "hustling for my worthiness." To some extent it did work. It wasn't until years later that I realized, with the aid of lots of self-help books and a great business coach, that I know that I am whole. I don't have to pretend to be whole. I am whole. This is the foundation upon which a successful negotiation must begin.

Mercifully, I was sent to boarding school for high school, then at 19, decided to "rebel" by getting married and dropping out of college. I had three children by the ripe old age of 23. I finally went back and finished my college degree and started teaching elementary school, and then at 29 years old woke up and found myself in a marriage that (not surprisingly – I mean who can pick a life mate at 19!) wasn't going well. I decided to divorce my then-husband and put myself back through law school at night.

I met my current husband in law school. We were married and eventually had one child together. When I graduated from law school at just over 30 years old, I still hadn't really lived in the adult world. As a teacher, there is no "negotiating" anything. Not the salary. Not the benefits. None of it. There is a step system and if you have a certain number of years of experience with a certain degree or other "incentives" then your pay is the pay. It's all contractual and everyone is treated exactly the same.

So by the time I was sitting in the law offices of the man who would become my first boss in the legal world, I was a babe in the woods. I had no armor, no skills and barely knew much about anything in the world. (I still thought white zinfandel wine was pretty good. Yup. Exactly.) I had already met with the man's law partner. She was also half Chinese and because she and I had hit it off so much, I thought this interview was simply a meet and greet. Boy, was I wrong.

He was a seasoned litigator, and very accustomed to making people squirm. A graduate of The Citadel, a Vietnam War veteran, and a southern aristocrat. Very much like the character Kevin Spacey played in House of Cards, he was steely and smooth as he deliberately laid his questions on me. His deposition skills finely honed, he grilled me as if I were being cross examined on the witness stand. Many of the questions were what you'd expect, asking about my law school classes and my prior work experience. What I didn't expect was this. He asked me why I was moving to the area where the law firm was (it was about 100 miles from where my husband and I attended law school). I told him that my boyfriend (now husband, who had graduated a year ahead of me) had already started working there; that he'd accepted a job as a state attorney in that area. He then proceeded to say, "So you're just moving here to follow your boyfriend." I really didn't know how to respond. Every answer ran through my brain at the same time. "Yes?" "No?" "None of your business?" I was so surprised by that question at the time. Looking back now as I have now been an employer and owned my own law firm, I realize that he probably was, not so tactfully, wondering what would happen if my then boyfriend and I broke up – would I then go scurrying back from whence I came? But alas, anyway, I was offered the position but as a fresh-faced graduate, having seemingly nothing with which to bargain, and certainly not one scintilla of negotiating skills, I grabbed the first offer they threw my way, and asked only when I could start!

Sheryl Sandburg, in her book *Lean In*, very honestly tells the story of when she was offered the position of Chief Operating Officer for Facebook. She was so excited to get that offer, and was poised to just accept, when a male friend of hers, who had no idea what the terms of her offer were, deftly asked why she would take any less than any man would have in her position. Confused at first, she then realized what he was conveying to her. No man would simply take the first offer. Taking her friend's advice, she went back to Mark Zuckerberg and Facebook with a fair counteroffer. She then spent the entire weekend basically vomiting and having a panic attack that she had quite possibly thrown away one of the best job offers she may ever receive. But guess what? Facebook accepted her counteroffer and the rest became history. She learned a very valuable lesson. She learned how to assert her value and be unflinching about it.

Knowing your value comes from within not without. For so many of us, this is one of those many really annoying life lessons that is way easier said than done. That little voice inside your head, the one whom I call "IT", is a stubborn little asshole. Some call it your inner critic, others have other choice names, but we all have that little brat in there that tells us we aren't good enough, we aren't smart enough, thin enough, pretty or handsome enough, or maybe that we just plain aren't good, period.

That voice wreaks havoc when we must step up to the plate and ask for something. That's when the old Wayne's World chorus turns up the volume in our heads and screams, "You're not worthy. You're not worthy." Then many of us hear that and go, "oh that's right! What was I thinking???," before slinking back into our seats of shame and slithering into what we hope is invisibility. It's an uncomfortable seat for sure, but that call of familiarity is all too enticing. It feels safer than throwing ourselves onto the court.

The thing we all have is a way that the world "occurs" for us, the way we see things. That way of seeing the world can be vastly different depending on what your experiences have been. As we move through life, we don't often think about how the world may be occurring for others. We simply assume that it is the same for everyone. If we didn't think that, then there would be far less judgment. Admit it, how often do you think, "how could they do that??" The truth is that there is no real truth. Law of attraction guru and spiritual teacher, Esther Hicks says that a belief is just a thought you've been thinking over and over again.

We humanoids, burst on the scene of Planet Earth, in a very vulnerable state. We can't see, can't walk, can't feed ourselves, and can't speak. We are literally, figuratively and completely dependent upon others for survival. From there, we are shaped and molded by our experiences and interactions. Then we created habits and drew conclusions. And those conclusions are often misplaced but we march along as if they are true then look for evidence in reality that they are true. Then because of the basic principle of physics that like attracts like, you will find that evidence. This is not unlike the phenomenon that many of us have experienced which is once you buy a yellow car, you start seeing yellow cars on the road everywhere you go.

A really good example of a misplaced conclusion is the example of a baby in a crib. The baby's crib has a mobile on it which turns and plays music for them. One day, while lying there, the baby kicks his feet into the air while the mother happens to be turning on the mobile. He then draws the conclusion that his kicking his feet caused the mobile to turn on. Then later on, it happens again. Now he is certain that kicking his feet is what turns on the mobile. Obviously, that is not how the mobile turns on, but he thinks it is.

In life it is much more serious than the baby and the mobile in the crib. I have a friend who went through life thinking she wasn't loveable because one time, when she was five years old, she saw her aunt holding her two sisters on her lap, so she ran over there to jump on her aunt's lap too. At that moment, her aunt cried out that there were too many kids on her lap and made everyone jump off. In that moment, she decided she wasn't worthy. Now any adult could see that situation for what it was

– a person who just didn't want three kids burying her – that it had absolutely nothing to do with the value of the third kid who wanted to pile on – but the little girl took it as a definition of her value and spent the rest of her life proving that she had value in other ways. It all seems so silly when we know she had value to begin with and didn't need to prove anything at all. But the reality is the little girl represents millions of us who drew mistaken conclusions as children and then built a lifetime around those erroneous conclusions.

The conclusions can vary widely but they all share a common theme of thoughts that don't serve us. The inner demon may tell you that you're not capable, that the world isn't fair, that you can't get what you want, that you aren't likeable, not pretty, not the right shape, color, size, or yada yada yada. When you think those thoughts long enough, they become a habit you believe is YOU, rather than just thoughts you've had for most of your life.

Dr. Joe Dispenza has written several books around this topic, and he explains the actual neuroscience that makes up the thing you call "you." He explains that "you" are actually consciousness. We are a soul that is the electricity that turns on the bag of skin and bones we walk around in. It is a basic principle of physics that energy is neither created nor destroyed, which means that the energy of our souls does not die when our bodies disintegrate and eventually turn to dust. That energy has to go somewhere. Now, consider that energy is not inherently bad or good. It just is. That means that YOU, the energy of

YOU is not bad or good. It simply is. I had a business coach once who said, life is empty and meaningless, and it is empty and meaningless that it is empty and meaningless. Kind of sounds circular, but what it means is that WE are the ones that add meaning to everything. We are meaning making machines! Someone looks at us funny and it immediately sends us on a spiral of why, and we proceed to make up an elaborate story of what it means, when it might actually mean nothing at all!

What you think is "you" are actually just a creation you didn't consciously become. Your thoughts were haphazardly conjured in your mind, without deliberate choice, planning, structure, organization or intent. It's like a homeless person who wanders around and gathers cans to turn in for money but only grabs them up if they happen to see them. They are not planning their lives. Life is happening to them.

You, the real you, are actually consciousness. That consciousness is absolutely perfect. Yes, there is a part of you that is actually perfect. This consciousness is totally separate from the emotions we experience. The emotions are actually just rockets of energy fired by the brain out into the physical body. Our brains have a direct connection to the physical body. We know this because if we get scared, our hearts start racing and feel as if they are beating out of our chests; if we are nervous, we start to sweat; if we are sad, we start to cry. All of these are physical manifestations of emotions that started in our brains and by experiencing the thoughts, millions of cells in our brains become activated and start rapid firing electrical currents throughout the body through the neuronal pathways. It is not unlike turning on a particular switch in your house, it lights up a particular room.

Just like there are ways to make the electricity circuits in your house more efficient, your brain is also wired to be more efficient. It also detests uncertainty. It wants to predict. In order to do that, the neurons start creating a latticework of patterns. The more you think certain thoughts over and over again, the groove of that particular latticework of patterns continues to be deepened and etched. Over time, as you grow from being a child into an adult, and even into adulthood, you are forming and continuing to mold and shape these neuronal patterns. Everything you think is "you" – your dreams, feelings and memories – are all actually neuronal patterns.

The brain's efficiency takes it a step even further than that. When certain stimuli are presented to you that your brain recognizes as being similar to something else you've already experienced in the past, and especially once you've formed deep neuronal patterns around that area, the reaction will be instantaneous. This means that if you had a mean older female teacher as a child, then you might have an immediate and visceral reaction to an older female boss as an adult. You might not even recognize it. You might just think you don't like that boss. But you've actually mentally rehearsed that scenario over and over and over again.

The 'you" that you think is you is really an "IT" – not your authentically created self but a made-up self that you can actually change. In other words, you are not inherently "unworthy." You can't take an x-ray and see unworthy right there next to your liver – that state of alleged "unworthiness" lives inside your brain as neurons firing together in a particular latticework pattern. You have the ability to totally destroy that pattern and create a new one.

What does all of this mean when you are trying to get something you want? It means you carry around that latticework of 100 billion brain cells with you wherever you go. It means that when you fear rejection, your fears are likely based on your interactions over the years. The crazy thing is that the other person may convey something to you that they think is perfectly innocuous but sends your neuronal patterns on into a firestorm of emotions.

The bottom line is that your "worth" is tied up in these neuronal patterns. It is literally "hard-wired". That's the (sort of) bad news. The really good news is that just as you created the patterns, you can recreate them – and this time you can do consciously. So if you think you are inherently not worthy – it's simply not the case. You can change your thoughts and your brains by training them to think different thoughts.

Our thoughts all originate in our frontal lobe. The "you" that you think is "you" resides in that frontal lobe. Your frontal lobe can be molded, and shaped and changed so that the "you" that you think is "you" can become an entirely different "you." You can navigate your future this way, control your behavior, and dream of new possibilities. This means you can reshape your brain and therefore your future.

People Will Think What You Tell Them to Think

Years ago, I had left the practice of law for a period of time and dabbled in the profession of being a financial advisor. I got my Series 7 and 66 licenses and went to work for Northern Trust, and later Morgan Stanley. After a couple of years in that profession, I had a divorce attorney friend come to me and tell me that she was relocating to another city and wanted to know if I wanted her practice. It was very small, but it was a great runway for me to get my own practice going, so I took her up on her offer.

It was around this time that I first hired the business coach who I have now worked with off and on for many years. I told her I was afraid that people in the community were going to think I didn't know what the heck I wanted. I had been a lawyer, then a financial advisor then back to being a lawyer. After my little rant about that, my coach gave me advice that I never, ever forgot and continue to use in my daily life every day. That is – people will think what you tell them to think.

She then went on to tell me what I was going to tell people to think. I was going to tell them to think I was the only family law attorney in town who had a financial background; that I was better equipped than any other divorce lawyer at looking at portfolios, and determine how much income they could generate, and helping people with protecting their lifestyles and wallets going forward. So that's how I marketed myself, and lo and behold, I can't tell you how many clients sat in their initial consultations and told me that they wanted me in particular because I was the only divorce attorney who had a financial background. Yup. People will think what you tell them to think.

The negotiation paradox is this. The fear of being disliked or rejected actually makes it more likely that we will experience that phenomenon from others. We send out those rockets of energy that people can sense and then that's what comes back to us. There is a science behind this principle too. We have something called mirror neurons. It is why when someone yawns, we yawn too. In babies, we see this when one starts crying, then another one will start crying. It also is the reason why it is way more fun to laugh together. We see someone laughing and it makes us also want to laugh. These mirror neurons are found in animals as well as humans. They cause us to mirror the behavior of another and act it out as our own. We can use these mirror neurons to our advantage by conveying our thoughts and our value to other people with whom we are interacting.

Therefore, in determining your value, you not only get to define it, you can convey that value to the world. We see this in successful people all the time. Will Smith once said, "I've always been an A-List actor; you just didn't know it yet." Stevie

Nicks said once that when she was 18 years old and a student at San Jose State University, she would dress up in her coolest rock star outfits and strut across the middle of the campus and think "Don't you people know who I am? I'm a rock star!" The value starts within. In some ways it is counterintuitive. Often, we subconsciously think that once the world starts valuing us, then we will feel our value. Let me tell you, as long as you are looking to the outside world to create your internal value, you will always, always come up short.

Inventing Your New Self

You can choose to create the self that you are and then that created self will be the authentic self. The key is that your brain must know with every cell and every neuron that you are that new self. You must become it – not like mastering it – like an actor does his lines – but just as much as you feel like a man or a woman – this becomes the "you" that you are. When you wake up in the morning, you don't have to remind yourself of your gender. You just are that gender. You don't say to yourself, "well if I'm a man that means I shave my face." or "well if I'm a female, that means I put on makeup." You just are those things. This is exactly how you will feel inside of your created self.

Time to Take Out the Head Trash

In order to make real changes and really get rid of that inner critic and FEEL your internal value, you have to take out the trash thoughts that are sitting in your brain now and replace them with fresh, new thoughts that will serve you. These replacement thoughts will serve you in negotiation and assist you with getting what you want, but also serve you in the rest of your life too. It is a process and will feel a little painful at first but will definitely be worth it in the end. Think of it as a debridement. When a surgeon has to "debride" a wound, it sounds and is super gross, but they actually get in there and cut away all of the dead, damaged tissue and foreign objects that may be in there, so that healthy tissue has the space to grow. From this process, total healing takes place.

You want to get what you want? You want to feel as if you matter in a negotiation? The Go point, the Starting Point for this game is very close to you. It is inside your head. We start right inside your brain.

"Rewiring" Your Brain

The concept of rewiring your brain seems new but it has been around for centuries. Forward thinking scientists such as DaVinci, Galileo, and Einstein all proffered concepts of quantum mechanics in their writings and their work and also lived by those principles. The thoughts which fire in our brains are energy and that energy can be controlled. In order for you to feel your value then assert it with confidence, so people will acknowledge that you matter, it is essential that you understand some basic concepts. Einstein said it best when he said:

*Everything is energy and that's all there is to it. Match the frequency of the reality you want and you cannot help but get that reality. It can be no other way. This is **not** philosophy. This is **physics**.*

Our brains are comprised of three parts. The base of the brain, also sometimes called the lizard brain, is the oldest part of our brains and keeps us alive. It controls the involuntary functions that we need to stay alive but that we don't want to have to remember to do – like beating your heart and breathing. The frontal lobe, which is about 40% of the brain, is what we think of as ourselves. That's where all of our conscious thinking takes place. If we were computers, this would be the CPU. This area of the brain has connections to all other parts of your brain. So when you have a thought or an idea that is originated in the frontal lobe, it will immediately send signals to the rest of your brain. You have a thought, then your CPU looks out over the entire network then calls upon the various networks of neurons that are stored in your brain, based on something you've learned intellectually – knowledge; or something you've experienced in your life. This means that if you see an ice cream truck, your brain sends a signal to a certain network of neurons that have been woven together to remember that you loved hearing the ice cream truck bells as a child, and you would run to get in line, then get your toasted almond bar. It's all automatic.

When you have a new idea, the CPU will then take the networks of neurons that are already in your brain and seamlessly piece them together to create that new idea – a new vision - and when you merge the networks together, they fire in a new pattern, and that's when you'll get a clear picture in your mind. We call that new picture your "intentions".

The more specific your vision is of your new intention, the more likely it is that it will come into physical being in your world. For example, you can picture the word "career". Once you see that vision clearly, then you start to live that dream and it starts being a living motion picture. It works for things you don't want also. If you picture "jobless" and focus on what it would be like to lose your job then that is your living motion picture instead. The moment you light that fire with a thought, it starts taking on form and time in all the things you're going to do. You're now actually living in that future. Here's the really mindblowing part. At that point, your brain does not know the difference between the actual event that is taking place in your life and the future you are imagining in your mind (mental rehearsal). You are literally rewiring your brain to be your future self!

Once you have been able to master controlling those thoughts, your brain will no longer be a record of the past but rather will become a map to the future. Most people stop at this level and then wonder why their lives haven't changed. You can't just create a vision board and expect things to manifest.

There is another level which is actually just as critical. What gives your intentions life is combining them with emotions. You have to feel with every ounce of your being that you are that new person. You have to know it and have passion about it. That's when the universe starts to really bring you everything you want, including WHO you define yourself to be. It's like water. It flows right to your door and when that happens, you see your thoughts actually begin to change your cells on a granular level in preparation for your created future.

This can be a bit difficult. For people who think that "someday" you will feel better or someday your level will improve. You are in a way of being that says you don't have it now, but you will "someday." In order for you to manifest your new self now, you have to believe that that is who you are now. Not "someday" but TODAY. You can't wait to be totally healed in order to feel that wholeness – or that value. You will absolutely need that feeling of value before you start negotiating, if you're going to negotiate from a place of strength. In other words, you have to feel that value and wholeness first, in order to destroy the old neuronal pathways and create new ones. Most people wait for something outside of them to happen to feel better but it is the other way around. Think of a cause and the effect of that cause. You get to be the cause of your reality – not the effect of it. But in order to effectuate that change and see the newly created future showing up in your present life, you are

41

going to have to change how you think and how you feel before the experience occurs in order for your new life to find you.

Your present personality – that set of neuronal pathways – has created your present experience of what you perceive as your life. If you want to effectuate a change in perception of your self-worth and thus, your value, you'll have to become conscious of unconscious habits and behaviors and thoughts that aren't serving you, and modify them.

The key is to look at your habits, habits about your value and your self-worth in the past and decide if those thoughts, feelings and beliefs belong in your future. You can't try to create a new reality on top of the old neuronal patterns. It's like taking a band aid and putting it on a broken arm. Doesn't work. You have to actually have the doctor go in and reset the bones, put them into place, then hold them into place, until they start growing in a certain way.

In order to feel your value now, you have to start envisioning yourself as worthy now. It sounds counterintuitive but that's how you will start to reprogram your brain. A concrete example of this is that a wealthy person doesn't feel lack. That's not how the wealthy person created wealth. They created wealth by feeling wealthy. The real work in this piece is that you have to be super vigilant, stay conscious and be paying attention to who you're being all the time. You can't let any thoughts slip by your awareness, because if you do, then like a Jack-in-a-Box, your old self will pop right back up. To protect yourself against this from happening, you can't react emotionally to things that cause you to feel like the old self, and you can't blame or complain. Once you allow your old habitual way of thinking to creep back in, your new future is pushed away. The key is to hold that state of mind for long periods of time so that your new self and your new future join with your present. This part only happens with continuous repetition. You are destroying old neuronal pathways and creating new ones.

Don't beat yourself up if you aren't successful all the time at first. When I began this process, I had to remind myself constantly of the new "me" that I was creating. I had to have conversations inside my head such as "who just had that thought?" MmmHmmm. Exactly. Trash please. You are actually teaching your body how your future self will be feeling, responding and acting. The real test is whether you can maintain that new sense of self the whole day – independent of any other person, or thing that happens, and independent of any emotional addiction.

Even when you're a master at this, there always will be a dance between your free will consciousness and the consciousness that's embedded deep inside your brain. Sometimes you just have to have a conversation with your inner person, "IT," and tell him or her, "hey! Listen, I'm working on this – I know you're not real. I know you are just neuronal patterns and thoughts that are just clusters of energy that have learned to fire together. So,

I'm acknowledging that you're there but you're not real so I can look past you. BEGONE!"

One of my favorite Seinfeld vignettes was an exchange between Kramer and George, and Kramer says to George, "what does the little man inside you say?" and George says, "Ohhh, my little man is an IDIOT!" Sometimes that little troll inside your head says really idiotic things. Time to shut that down.

Make a Decision

The word decision means a conclusion or resolution reached after consideration. It is from an old French word *decider* which was from the Latin word *decider* "to decide, determine," literally "to cut off," from *de* "off" + *caedere* "to cut."

In my first book, *Breaking Free: A Step by Step Guide to Achieving Emotional, Physical and Spiritual Freedom,* I talked about how you can decide what your life will look like, then declare it so. We can do that with outcomes of conversations in which we want to persuade someone to do what we want them to.

A declaration is more than just a powerful statement. It is the first step in creation. Everything that has ever come into existence has begun with a declaration. When Orville and Wilber Wright declared that they were going to invent a contraption that would fly people in the sky, no one thought it was possible. It had never been done. When our forefathers, Thomas Jefferson, John Adams, Benjamin Franklin and their contemporaries decided to create a new country, they were viewed as renegades and treasonous. Imagine if a few guys got together today and said, "We are going to start our own country!" Would you think that they were crazy?

In the book, *The Four Agreements*, Don Miguel Ruiz references the Bible, and how it begins. It begins by saying that "in the beginning there was the word and the word was God". We can harness that power of word to create anything we want through our declarations. Just as our forefathers declared that there would be a new country when there were only 2.5 million people living here, you can also declare your chosen life into existence.

Wayne Dyer said that just using the two words, "I am" is extremely powerful. He said that since childhood there has been a conditioning of our minds in the realm of "I am not". Our self-talk is often very unkind. If self-talk had a name it would have "Bully" in it somewhere. We often find ourselves saying things to ourselves like "I am not smart enough", "I am fat", "I am not pretty enough", "I am not strong enough", "I am not likeable" and the poisonous list goes on and on. Eventually, you start to believe this voice. Then you start to see evidence of it in reality, so you think, "See! Self-Talk a/k/a Bully is right!" Like trick mirrors, this is one of the tricks that Self-Talk a/k/a Bully plays on you. The evidence in reality does not come first and then your mind sees it and knows that whatever you are seeing is real. The truth is that it is actually the other way around. First, your mind thinks whatever it is, then it shows up in your world.

History is replete with highly evolved souls who have known this truth and have spoken it. Buddha has said "The mind is everything. What you think you become." Psychologists have called it a "self-fulfilling prophecy." From a purely physical stance, your thoughts are energy. A thought will form in your brain and ignite physical and biological waves of energy which begin to emit into the world. Just as you can feel the warmth of a fire even though you can't "see" the warmth, you know it is there because you can feel the warmth emitting from it. While you can't "feel" the warmth of your thoughts or "see" them emitting energy, they are sending messages out into the universe and into your world. Your thoughts then set about setting up your world to match accordingly. It is a mirror back to you, not the other way around. So, you see if you realize this, then you realize that it is not possible for your world to be created in any way other than the way you have ordered it to be through your thoughts.

If you decide that your world is chaotic, that you are terrible with money, that you are terrible at relationships and always pick the wrong person for yourself, then your thoughts set about creating that reality for you. Your thoughts are like little worker elves who run out into the world upon your command and do as you have instructed. They know nothing else than to carry out the wishes of their master. Thus, there is no way that you will think those thoughts and then magically have a world that is peaceful, have you being excellent with money, great in relationships and having chosen the right person.

When you declare, there are no "qualifying" types of words. There are no phrases tacked onto a declaration such as "I hope" or "Maybe this will happen" or "It would be nice" or "I will try". A declaration is a commanding statement made with complete conviction that it will happen. Remember your worker elves cannot understand qualifying words – they only understand commands. Martin Luther King understood the power of declaration when he delivered his now famed and celebrated "I Have a Dream" speech. He stood up in front of millions of people and declared his dream. His speech would have not even been memorable had he said "I have a dream that I hope that maybe someday people will judge my children on the content of the character, maybe if you want to, instead of the color of their skin, even though I doubt that is ever going to happen."

Words have power. Your thoughts have power. They have this power with or without you having an awareness of it, but you have complete control once you are aware of it. In negotiation, the insidious kinds of statements a/k/a orders handed to your worker elves might sound like this:

"I hate conflict."

"I'm terrible at standing up for myself."

"I don't want to look greedy/selfish/difficult."

"I don't want to be rejected."

"I don't want to look like a fool."

I have a friend who would say, "Do you want to be right about that? Or would you like things to be different?" Decide today that you will harness this power and declare your choices about what you want and that you are going to realize it. One of my all-time favorite quotes is from "*Star Wars: The Empire Strikes Back*". In that scene Yoda is training a young Master Luke Skywalker to be a Jedi. At one point when Luke says, "All right, I'll give it a try", Yoda responds with "Try not. Do… or do not. There is no try." When you say, "I'll try" or "I hope", you might as well say "I am not doing this". The result is the same. In order for your declarations to have power, they must override the thoughts that have worn grooves into your brain. Those old grooves must be destroyed so that new ones can be built. Your worker elves have grown used to their old set of orders. You will have to remind them constantly that their old orders are no longer being used.

Declarations are not goals. They are not aspirational in nature. Goals might or might not be attained. Aspirations might or might not be realized. A declaration is a command to your world that this is how it is. Period. When you say, "I am a human being", you are sure that you are a human being. You don't think, "well, actually maybe I am a lion." You know it with every cell in your body. Your declarations are no different. Once you declare them, you have to know that they are real and true with every fiber of your being. Anything less and they have no power. So, if you want a different life, declare it. Feel it. Know it.

Feel the Fear Then Do It Anyway

When I lecture around the country on negotiation, I always ask people what holds them back from negotiating or what is it that paralyzes them about the process? The answers are universal, whether I am speaking in Florida, California, New York or Washington DC. At our very core, we are human beings and we are far more alike than we are different. As much as we like to think we are unique or that no one else could possibly understand what we are thinking or feeling, the reality is that every single person you know, you are connected to, or who you pass on the street, has the same needs and insecurities that you have.

We spend a whole lot of our time and energy protecting that scared little orphaned child who lives inside us. That little child works really hard at protecting itself from whatever it needs to, so lots of time is spent trying to look good and maybe even more time is spent trying to avoiding look bad.

The irony is that when you are afraid, people treat you with less respect, which is the very thing you were afraid of in the first place. When you approach a situation with full confidence, the other person responds in kind and treats you with more respect. When you face your fears head on and blow through them, your confidence level soars. Fear is just "False Evidence

Appearing **R**eal" anyway. Most of the time, that which was your worst fear doesn't even exist except in your mind.

Your Self Worth

Eleanor Roosevelt is credited as saying "no one can make you feel inferior without your consent." I have consistently taught my children, especially my daughters, not to allow anyone else to dictate how they will feel. The flip side of these thoughts brings us back to where we started with this chapter. That is that you, and you alone, define your value.

To understand and measure the baseline of feelings of self-worth that you have for yourself, consider this little test. For just a moment, imagine that the following has been stripped away from you:

- your job
- your career
- your house
- your money

What if everything that is of material value was taken from you, including anything that gives you a sense of prestige? Now, ask yourself how you feel at that point. That is your measure of self-worth. So many of us have our self-worth wrongfully intertwined with what we do for a living, how much money we have, who our friends are and on and on. That is a dangerous place to be because then if something catastrophic happens, you suddenly think you no longer have value. I once represented a guy who had lost nearly all of his entire fortune because it had been invested with Bernie Madoff. He expressed to me that he was contemplating suicide. He truly felt he was nothing without his money. After several months, he and his wife reconciled, and he learned that he has value even without the money. In fact, he actually began a relationship with the spiritual universe that continues to be strong today. Losing that money ended up being the best gift that could have ever been given to him, because through that loss he gained something so much more. His true self.

Create Your New "Self"

Years ago, when I first learned this process, I created a document called "Who Am I?" This was not so much a manifesto but an expression of who I truly longed to be and who I knew myself to be. I wrote out 10 things that I decided to create myself to be. They were all written in the form of "I am…" "I am" is a much more powerful statement than "I want to be…" or "I will be…" or "I will try to be…". You will want to do this too. Then memorize, memorize, memorize. Say them to yourself throughout the day, every day. This is the easiest way to destroy those old neuronal pathways

When you are creating yours, keep them general to various areas of your life because these are the foundation of who you are. Think in terms of who you are for yourself, then who you are in your relationships, who you are as a financial producer, who you are in terms of physical fitness and who you are as a spiritual being.

Your specific goals, say for business, are something that you will create separately but they rest on this foundation. My "Who Am I?" declaration has changed throughout the past ten years since I first started this process. You will also want to keep them updated and current as you change. As an example, here are what mine are now.

1. I am a powerful expression of what's possible for women, and for all people.
2. I am a conversation for possibility. When people are with me, they feel empowered and inspired.
3. I am confident, whole and complete and the living embodiment of integrity.
4. I am a role model for my children for what's possible.
5. I am a loving wife and mother, and have loving and healthy relationships with them and with everyone in my world.
6. I create resources which are a conduit for people to gain access to knowledge, methods and strategies, which empower them to live their lives authentically and to create new beginnings and new futures. These resources transform lives all over the world.

7. I am a remarkable "results producer," and I experience unprecedented breakthroughs in revenue, which continues to ignite my passion to empower others and to make a lasting difference.
8. My success as a professional allows me and my family to live comfortably and gives us the options to do the things we want to be able to do.
9. I am healthy and fit and take care of my body.
10. I take care of my mind, spirit and soul by meditating for at least a short period every day.

Once you have them set, then you start to live from this place. You have to then have the integrity to remain living from this place, no matter what. You brain network will want to hold on to the old habits for dear life. When you start introducing new stuff and trying to destroy the old, the brain will be screaming out at you "Hey, no way! That's not you! You don't want to try something new – that's super scary and you are terrible at that anyway!" You just will have to have a plan. You see those old thoughts that aren't serving you, you acknowledge that it is just the brain remembering, then watch them go past you and into the ditch. From there, they will be carried the sewer and out to sea. Poof. Gone.

Don't get me wrong. It can definitely be difficult. Once, when I still was transforming and rewiring my brain to be the person I had declared myself to be, I had to attend a Florida bar conference. I knew all the family law attorneys would be there. On the drive to the conference, old-not-serving-me thoughts starting bombarding. "I am terrible in peer situations because I am so different. I don't fit in." Well you get the picture. Honestly those thoughts are so foreign to me now that it is almost like writing about someone else. In a way, that actually was someone else because those neuronal pathways don't exist anymore. Well, when that flood of old thoughts came rushing in, I stopped them, mid wave, and said to them, "I know who you are and what you're doing, and that's not me. I am a powerful expression of what's possible, and powerful people don't have these thoughts." You literally have to filter your poisonous thoughts through your newly created declaration so that you start to live from that place.

Without Integrity, Nothing Works

When I was in sixth grade, my teacher, Mrs. Shea, gave me my first lesson about integrity. I had never even heard that word before that I recall. One day, we were supposed to have a big, scary test. Throughout the day, we kept thinking it was coming. By lunch, still no test. The minutes clicked by and still she didn't bring it up and so, neither did we. At 3:00 PM the bell rang, and we were dismissed! We all sprang up and bolted toward the door, none of us mentioning anything about the test that we were supposed to have taken that day.

The next morning, we quietly filed in, again with no plans to mention anything about the test. When we took our seats, Mrs. Shea quietly glided to the front of the class completely silent. She continued to remain uncomfortably silent as she picked up the chalk and began to write on the blackboard. Slowly she wrote only one word in all capitals… "I N T E G R I T Y". She then proceeded to define it for us, "Integrity is having high moral values and ethics." We took the test that day and got a dose of punishment along with it for good measure. Lesson learned.

Integrity does mean to adhere to a high standard of honesty, morals and values. It also means that something is structurally sound. From the Latin word *integer* which means being whole or complete, the word integrity is the foundation upon which we build our lives. In fact, I will suggest to you that without integrity, nothing in your life will work. Just as tendons and ligaments hold together your bones and muscles, integrity holds everything together in your life.

In virtually every area of your life, the opportunity to choose to operate with or without integrity is present. Integrity is making a choice to do the right thing, to honor your word to others and to yourself, and operating at your highest level of being. Choosing not to operate within the context of integrity is a choice to cheat others – that is clear. What is not as readily immediately apparent is that operating without the context of integrity is a choice to cheat *you*. While the effects may not appear immediately (sometimes they do), they will appear. Often, because there is a time lapse, the lack of integrity will not immediately materialize as such. The impact of that effect also is often a further perpetuation of a negative self-worth or self-esteem. This is where people begin to blame others because of the lack of workability in their personal lives, their workplace, and their finances.

Building your life upon a foundation that lacks integrity is the equivalent of the two little pigs who built their houses out of straw and sticks. One huff and puff and it will all come crashing down. Creating a life with integrity is building the brick house that the third little pig built. No amount of huffing and puffing from any big bad wolves will blow it over. When Lance Armstrong was interviewed, he recounted the web of lies he had carefully spun for years and years, and all I could think was how his life had been built without the benefit of the most important ingredient, integrity. So like the straw house, it all came crashing down. He lost his reputation, his accolades, and his endorsement contracts. His decision to operate with a lack of integrity came with tremendous personal and professional cost.

Integrity means doing the right thing, even when no one else is watching and no one might even ever find out. Like the principle in physics, for every action there is an equal and opposite reaction, your actions will cause an action back to you and if you have acted in a less than ethical or dishonest manner, the opposite reaction will not be pleasant. My father always used to caution us, "Be careful what you throw up in the air, it is liable to come back down and hit you in the head." Choosing not to honor your word or to be dishonest is a choice against yourself.

Once we declare who we are and what our life looks like, we become the alchemists of our lives, creating our world the way we want it to be by commanding it to be so. Our declarations are the bones and muscles to the integrity which is the ligaments and tendons. In order for the bones and muscles to operate together as a unit, the ligaments and tendons have to present to pull it all together. In order for our declarations to be successful, there must be a system of integrity.

Here is how it works (or doesn't work). Let's say that you have declared that you are whole and complete and that you interact with people as though they are whole and complete. You read it in the morning, have it in your car, have a reminder of that pop up on your phone, and have it in your office at your computer. Then one day, you spend an hour telling your spouse what a jackass he is, getting into specific details about all of his various shortcomings. Is this interacting with your spouse as if he is whole and complete? Clearly not. This is an excellent example of how you are making him wrong and you right. Interacting with others as though they are whole and complete is not making anyone wrong. You would therefore then be out of integrity with your own word.

Therefore, once you have made your declarations, you must have the integrity to stick to them. Otherwise, you are *out of integrity*. You are not honoring your word. Your words have awesome power. Respect the power of that word by knowing that once you declare something, it *is*. If you have declared that you are strong and confident, then feelings of insecurity are not who you are. Those feelings are felt by who you once were. You are strong and confident – if you are not that – then you are out of integrity – and without integrity, nothing in your life will work. With it, and your life is exactly as you declare that is.

EXERCISES:

1. Define who you are for yourself: (For example – I am a powerful expression of what's possible.)

   I am _____

   _____

   _____

   _____

2. Define who you are in your relationships:

   I am _____

   _____

   _____

3. Define who you are in your career: (For example – I am a confident and successful financial advisor, who has an incredible network of referrals, and my clients are high end professionals who appreciate the value of quality advice.)

   I am

   a _____, who _____

   _____, and __

   _____

   _____

   _____

   _____

_____

_____

4. Define who you are physically:

   I am _____

_____

_____

_____

_____

5. Define who you are as a spiritual being:

   I am _____

_____

_____

_____

_____

6. The thing I would like to have in my life that I will need to negotiate is:

_____

_____

_____

_____

_____

_____

7. The reason I want that is because:

_____

_____

_____

_____

_____

8. I believe I should have this because:

_____

_____

_____

_____

_____

Chapter 3 – "A" – Analyze Research and Create Arguments and Leverage

"Without data, you're just another person with an opinion."
~W. Edwards Deming

TAKEAWAYS FROM THIS CHAPTER:

- Doing your research in the areas of what it is that you want and determining your market value will give you the ammunition you need to argue your position successfully

- Figuring out what the other person's motivations are, what they will argue and being prepared to counter their positions is also key to winning your negotiation

- Create leverage and then determine the optimum time for using it

- Do a risk assessment once you've done all of your research before advancing the negotiation conversation

- Figure out your best and worst case scenarios and your "choke point" ahead of time and also create your first offer

- Determine the best place to have the negotiation conversation
- Time your *request* for the negotiation conversation, and the *actual* negotiation conversation so that it will ensure that you are heard and that the other person feels prepared to give you what you want

The next step in negotiation is determining your *extrinsic* value. This is the value that you have in the world. Once you know and feel internally that you are entitled to the highest possible level that you can achieve internally, now you have to take a look at your value in the world externally.

Remember that there is a difference. Your value internally has to do with your soul, your spirit, the whole and complete essence of who you are. Your value externally will be defined by your position in the world. For example, if you are a medical assistant. There will be a range of possibilities within the universe of what's available for a medical assistant in your area, at the size of your medical practice, at the type of your medical practice, for your years of experience and so forth. So while you absolutely, definitely want to create high visions here, you also can't just decide that you are an NBA player with a $20 million contract if you are 65 years old and 5 foot 4 inches tall.

Here is where you are going to be doing your research, analyzing it, forming your own arguments, determining what you think the other side's positions are going to be, preparing your responses to those positions, formulating your strategy, creating your leverage, figuring out what is incentivizing the other side (including their pain points) and establishing what your offers and choke point are going to be.

Research, Research, Research!

How important is research? In a word, very. It's everything. In a research study published by the Journal of Marketing Research, certain automotive repair merchants were asked if their customers' research influenced their final pricing. This is what they found:

- Car repair shops offered higher prices to callers who had not done proper research and thus, overestimated the price of the repair.
- Women were quoted a higher price than men.
- Either gender was quoted a higher price if they openly admitted they didn't know what the service ought to cost.
- Gender differences for price quotes were nonexistent when callers mentioned what they expected to pay—even if it was inaccurate—for the repair.
- Surprisingly, repair shops were *more likely* to offer a discount if asked to do so by a woman than by a man.

While this study was done with car repair merchants, it is safe to say that coming prepared to any negotiations, is going to be more persuasive. My father used to say, "whatever you say, say it with authority, and people will believe you." Take it from me, it is a whole lot easier to say things with authority, when you actually believe it and KNOW it too.

While you are doing your own research, take the time to step back and think about the situation objectively. Decide if you are making assumptions that may or may not be correct. Be open to possibilities that are different from your initial assumptions. Dig as deeply as you can.

Things you might want to research include:

- What is the market price for the product/service?
- What is the other party's normal price / what do they normally pay for the same product/service?
- How is their business doing?
- What is most important to them? (Price, timing, customer retention, customer satisfaction, etc.)

Research means a lot of different things in the context of negotiation. First, it means the obvious. If you are buying a car, get online and figure out how much the car would have cost the dealer, how much it is worth and how much a consumer should pay. If you want a pay raise, figure out comparable salaries or fees for your skill level and geographical area. If you are buying or selling a house, you will look at recent sales for homes in your area that are of similar size, bedrooms, bathrooms, location, and so forth. This is the kind of research people generally assume I am referring to when I say do your research.

By gathering your research, you are starting the process of formulating your arguments as to why your position is the stronger one. You will want the other side to consider your position and the more cold, hard facts you have to support your side, the better chance you have at prevailing and getting what you want. The key is not only to get what you want but to get the other side to give you what you want willingly. You want the other side to see the merits of your argument and feel that it makes sense.

If you have no buy-in from the other side, you are far less likely to come to an agreement, and even if you do, it is less likely to stick. People often change their minds, especially if they start thinking about the "deal" and start feeling how "unfair" they think it is. So, the more you can boost and strengthen your position with data, facts and figures, the better off you will be in the long run.

Understanding the Other Person's Position

The next part of this step, which is less obvious, is that you must do the other person's research. Yes, you heard me correctly. A master negotiator will do all of the research as if you are taking the other person's position in the negotiation. This means finding all the data, facts, figures and information that the other person would dig up if he or she were doing the same sort of thorough research that you will be doing.

Then you are going to anticipate every single argument the other side is either going to make or *could* make in order to support their position. So, you may be thinking, but what if they aren't thorough? Here's the thing. Even if the other side isn't as prepared, anticipating what their arguments will be, will only serve you. During the conversation, you will be able to say, "you may take the position that (x, y, z) and here is my response to that position." You'll be at the ready to refute any argument or position that they may take.

Research the Other Party

Find out all you can about the other side. If you will be negotiating with a group, an individual, a company, an association, or a professional – read everything you can find. You might even ask the other side if they have any marketing literature or other types of handouts about themselves, sent to you in advance. Check to see if the individual or entity has written or published articles or reports. Reading things that they have written may give you insight into their beliefs, positions and opinions. You may even want to talk to people who know information about the other side. Find out what kind of personality (ies) you're dealing with.

When you are thinking about what the other side is going to argue, what incentivizes them and what their positions are going to be, it is critical that you picture really being in their shoes. My law partner, Jack Long, has often said there's always three sides to every story: your side, the other person's side and the truth. What he means of course is that we all have our perceptions based upon how the world has unfolded to us. I have definitely come to realize that most people are doing the best they can and they truly believe that the way they see the world and the situations in it, is the right way.

In law school, I took a class called "Analysis of Evidence." (It is the class in which I met my current husband, actually!) That professor who was more English than the Queen of England, and older than John Gielgud, introduced the concept of "confabulation" to us. When a jury is presented with facts, they may "fill in" or assume certain events took place or facts which have not been introduced into evidence, or they may simply just remember the facts wrongly and make assumptions based upon their incorrect memories. In life, we all do the exact same thing. How many times has someone been short with you, and you are so certain that it has something to do with you? Then you are off on a trail of thinking that you knew that person was mean, or that he or she didn't like you, or that they don't like you because you are (insert blank) the wrong race, the wrong socioeconomic strata, the wrong gender, or the wrong religion. It might be that the person just heard their best friend was diagnosed with cancer, or that he or she is shy, or that they hate their job. Who knows? It more than likely has nothing to do with you.

In negotiations, how we perceive ourselves and the situations has everything to do with how we step up and have the conversation to try to persuade the other person to do something. In order to win, you will want to put yourselves directly in the other person's shoes, and figure out what it is that will make them feel as if they have mattered in this situation.

Learn What Motivates the Other Side

Figuring out what is motivating the other side will be key. Oftentimes, it isn't totally obvious, but if you really observe what the other side is saying and how they are behaving, it usually isn't too hard to determine. Key motivators are often not winning the actual argument that they are proffering but could be something more elusive such as pride or simply winning for winning's sake. It could be just to not let you win, or to see you suffer. While you might think these types of incentives are ridiculous or meritless, if they are indeed what is motivating the other side, then you will have to figure out a work-around in order to get what it is that you want.

Sales trainers often talk about "pain points." A pain point is an area in which a potential customer might be experiencing a problem. Therefore a manufacturer or a provider of services will want to speak to those areas of pain and offer solutions to their problems. By demonstrating that their problems can be solved with what they are selling, the potential purchaser or consumer is more likely to buy what they are selling. Negotiations are a form of sales. I actually say that everything you do is a form of sales. You want to identify the other person's pain points and then design solutions in the negotiation that will resolve those problem areas for them. Pain points are actually useful in two ways – one, they are what you can use to create leverage, and two, you will want to be sure that you design a resolution that brings relief to those pain points.

I once had a client who, after 12 hours of mediating and at 9 PM at night, just before signing a marital settlement agreement, while he was holding the signature pen, declare that he wasn't going to sign unless the wife gave him the cufflinks that the wife's father had given him on their wedding day. He said he wanted the cufflinks or $5000! I gave him the death stare but that didn't sway him. So, I then proceeded to ask him if the cufflinks were even worth $5000. I figured that might be a good place to start to see if this was a complete stab in the dark. Laughing at my silly attempt to dabble in reason, he unabashedly said "Nope, and I don't care. Cufflinks or $5000 or I don't settle the case."

So, what was driving him at this point do you think? Was it money? No. Was it that he really loved those cufflinks? Methinks not. Was it just to give one last dig to the wife on his way out? You betcha. The wife came back first with the idea that she give them to the husband and he agree to give them to the son when he turned 18. HIs response? "I'll see you at trial." (That's a no.) So the wife, who saw what he was trying to do and reasonably came to the conclusion that going to trial would have cost her far more than $5000, relented. Since she was not my client, I had no conversations with her about this issue, but I am certain that while it was a bitter pill to swallow, she concluded that by giving him this last moment, he got what he wanted and she would also get what she really wanted- her freedom! So, she gave him the $5000.

My client's "pain point" was that he felt the wife had devalued him. He knew that she treasured those cufflinks so he went after them. By giving in to the husband's seemingly ridiculous demand, she solved his problem and she was able to keep the cufflinks. While she didn't want to have to give him $5000, she also didn't want to have to spend more than that going to trial on the entire case. In the end, he felt valued by getting the $5000 and she got want she wanted: her freedom.

Determine Your Best and Worst Case Scenarios

Once you have done all of your research, researched the other side and figured out what is incentivizing the other side, then you can go to the next step in defining your value, which is to figure out what is your best case scenario and your worst case scenario. This is where you determine what the universe is that you are looking at for your particular situation.

Your best-case scenario is where you get everything you could possibly get. Now, I am all about the law of attraction and visualization and using the power of your word to get what you want. That being said, when you are doing all of that, keep in mind that adding a pinch of reality in your mix as you are stirring your recipe of what you want isn't a bad thing either.

What I mean by that is this. There have been times in my world, where a client might want more in alimony each month than the other person actually earns. You might also want to negotiate to be the starting quarterback for your favorite NFL football team, but you are a paunchy, balding 52-year-old, who hasn't worked out in 25 years. So your best-case scenario means your best case within the confines of your particular situation.

Then figure out what your worst possible scenario would be. This is where you think about what the situation will be if everything goes wrong and you get the bare minimum. Also be realistic here and incorporate all of the research and information that you've gathered.

At this juncture, it is critical you realize this…. Your best case? That's the other person's worst case. Your worst case? That's the other person's best case. Guess what? Nobody is settling for their worst-case scenario – which means that you are not getting your best case either. Unless you can figure out a way to sell your position so hard to the other side that they think they got something out of it, you need to start off the conversations with an offer something in the range of your best case scenario, but then figure out ahead of time what it is that you are going to be willing to let go.

Looking at the best/worst case scenario in terms of the matter/value paradigm, if one party gets everything that they want and the other party gets nothing, then one party will definitely feel that he or she didn't matter, wasn't valued and wasn't "seen." Because of that, either there will be no resolution, or if there is, the agreement will definitely be subject to challenge.

Risk Assessment

Once you have done all your research, then it is time to determine whether or not it is even worth having the conversation. This is a slippery slope, because your old voice, that little inner "IT" or inner "idiot" may try to speak up here and drown out the voices of reason. You will have to shush that old voice, make sure your inner voice that you've created, the one that tells you that you are whole and complete and have value, is the one that is speaking.

Then take a look at your research and make a calculated decision. If you have enough leverage, enough value to offer the other person, enough value to justify what you are asking for in terms of what you want for yourself, then you go for it. Sometimes these conversations might come forth only by virtue of a lawsuit being filed. If that is the case, then you will want to figure out what the return will be on your investment of time, attorney's fees, and aggravation.

Once you have considered all of the above then you can proceed to the rest of the preparation. The next step is to take a look at each one of the issues and grouping them in a way that you will be presenting them in terms of offers.

The Best Defense is a Strong Offense

An important note to interject here is something I have said for many years… that *if your only case/argument is what's wrong with the other side, then you have no case/argument.* You can and will want to pick apart the other side, but only as your secondary strategy. The strongest place to be is to have your own strong case.

It can be very tempting to focus in on what's wrong with the other side, what the other side has done wrong, or why the other side is weak. Those are all great arrows to have in your quiver. But if they are your only arrows, you will likely lose.

First, focus on *your* arguments, why your position is the strongest one, why your arguments are the soundest, and why you should prevail. Then move on to determining why the other side's weaknesses.

Keep Issues Separate

As you go through and identify the areas to be discussed, make sure to have each area as a separate item. You may use each as leverage in your negotiations, but it is important to be clear about each and every item you will be discussing.

Once you have isolated each of the areas, then identify objectives for each of the issues. This is where you will be figuring out the range or realm of possibilities for how your issues will be resolved. The minimum or worst case is the point at which you would walk away from the offer if the other party can't meet your request. The optimum or best case is your starting point – the best deal, one you see as ideal but something that is not outrageous. You don't want the first offer to be so offensive that the other side just shuts down or walks. The target range is the point where you would like to end up after negotiations.

Determine Your "Choke Point"

I was preparing a client for mediation one time and after walking her through her best- and worst-case scenarios, I then explained that we needed to figure out ahead of time what her "choke point" would be. This is my terminology for what your "walk away" point will be. My client said, "oh then, 'vomit point' may actually be a better word for it!" Funny, but true sometimes.

It is so much easier though, to make all these determinations before you walk into the room. The day of the negotiations can be stressful and depending upon who is on the other side, it can be very emotional. The better the other person knows you, the more likely it is they also know how to push each one of your buttons. Even if the other person isn't trying to push your buttons, things they say, mannerisms they have, ways they act, can all set you off. By being fully prepared, you are much less likely to be triggered.

Your choke point is the point that you determine ahead of time is going to be your bottom line. When you reach that bottom line and the offer has been rejected, or the other side offers something that is below that bottom line, then you know that you are finished with the conversation. It is at that time that you stand, politely state that the conversation is no longer productive, thank them for their time then excuse yourself. The trick here is that you have to be *ready* to walk away, and then *actually* do that.

Create Leverage But Don't Give It Away Too Early (AKA How to Deal With a Narcissist)

What is leverage? Leverage is the information that you hold which incentivizes the other side to want to resolve your dispute. It is a key element in negotiating. For example, the person who has the more urgent desire to get the case settled has less leverage than the person who doesn't care if the case ever get settled. You want to not only have as much leverage as you can going into the negotiation, you want the other side to feel that leverage. As the author Eoin Colfer has aptly stated, "The trick to negotiation is to hold all the cards going in and, even if you didn't, to try to look as though you do."

For some people, particularly women, or others who think leverage means "game-playing" – this may be a difficult topic. Many people will say to me that they don't want to fight or that they don't want to appear greedy, or just that they simply don't want to play games. They believe they can just talk things through. This may absolutely be the case with the chosen few rational people who also happen to agree on how things should be resolved. But for most people, you have to give them the incentive to settle and that incentive is called "*leverage*".

The bottom line is that every single person who has come through the doors of my office has said to me that they don't want to fight. While there are some who thrive on conflict, the majority of people don't like conflict and so creating leverage in not part of their regular DNA. For those people, creating leverage might feel underhanded or just sort of manipulative. But what it really comes down to is basic psychology – people need to feel is if they were given something. They also want what they think they can't have. In addition, some people really just want to win, no matter what the game is. These principles are particularly true if you are dealing with a person who has narcissistic tendencies or is a high conflict personality in general.

Remember that a narcissist at his or her core is a damaged personality that, underneath it all, has the worst case of self-loathing, the lowest self-esteem. For that personality type, the *only* thing that brings value is the external. But narcissists aside, let's face it, we've all played that losing game. Brené Brown, the shame and vulnerability expert explains it this way: "You either walk inside your story and own it or you stand outside your story and hustle for your worthiness." So, when negotiating, what's happening is a huge hustle for worthiness. The one who needs to win at all costs just to use that external validation as a salve on his or her damaged internal psyche is the biggest hustler of them all. That person, my friends, is your narcissist.

Guess what that means? That means you will never, ever win if you think you're going to win by getting more in the traditional sense. What I mean by more, is more of anything that may be of value to the narcissist. The way to beat them at their own game is by creating leverage and then strategically creating a first offer that includes far more than what you're willing to settle for.

How do you get leverage? First, you have to know the value of what you have that the other side might want. Central to this, you need to know what the other side wants. What are their pain points? What do they need or want? In certain negotiations such as in divorce, or with someone you know well, it is easier to figure out what is driving the other side. But no matter who you're dealing with, the first thing you should try to gage is what emotional investment the other side is investing into this conversation.

The second thing to do in order to gain leverage is to DO YOUR RESEARCH AND BE PREPARED. Figure out the value of things. For examples, you might need to do appraisals or get valuations. Know your facts. As discussed above, figure out what the other side might argue on these issues. Be prepared to meet that argument. While you may not win every point, you should know the strengths of your case and be prepared for the weaknesses.

Third, figure out what is incentivizing the other side. Is it money? Time with the kids? Pride? Looking good to the outside world? Winning? Beating you? Sometimes, the other side just wants to have the conversation over with or just be done having to deal with this issue. Taking some time to try to analyze what is driving and motivating the other side is critical.

Always remember that what is incentivizing you is not necessarily what is incentivizing the other side. Remember that the world occurs for each person differently depending on how life has unfolded for them. What might be completely innocuous to you is totally offensive to someone else.

Timing is Everything with Leverage
The next key element, now that you have identified your leverage, is to NOT GIVE IT AWAY TOO EARLY IN THE GAME. You'll want to be sure you are saving your leverage for when you are going to need it. I once had a male client who made this fatal mistake. It was a highly contested, overly litigated family law matter (overly litigated because the parties couldn't stop themselves from continuing the battle). The soon-to-be-ex-husband, who was my client, was still living in the

marital residence and the future-former-wife had moved out. However, when she moved out, she left her old cell phone in the home. This is an example of a marital asset that was left at the home, which was also a marital asset. He plugged in the phone, and there were all sorts of incriminating texts and emails. These were excellent trial exhibits for our case. (Side note: please remember that every text, every email, anything you ever put in writing – is a potential trial exhibit! So if you wouldn't want the judge to read it, don't hit "send").

So my client emails us all of these very useful texts and emails, then that night, during the middle of the night when he couldn't sleep, and he started drinking wine and was all alone stewing on these texts and emails (DANGER, DANGER – don't drink and text), he sent all of them over to her with his choice words. Translation – he took his great leverage and handed it right on over to the other side. This gave her the opportunity to be prepared, to spin them, to have an explanation and basically take all the wind from the sails of what could have been fantastic leverage.

The key in all of this is to have a clear idea of what you want, then to build a strategy on how to get there and employ the right tactics along the way. It is really important to have a true understanding of what you do want out of the resolution and what you can live without as you negotiate. So many people skip over this step or don't put enough thought into this.

Take time to prepare before approaching a negotiation. Start with assessing your own goals. One of the biggest mistakes I've seen, in my own negotiations and in those of others, is people coming in with a specific demand. For example, you may think you want the biggest office with the fabulous view, but you might not realize that it has a mold issue and the air conditioning doesn't work, so there might be a better tactic. You want to be ready to be flexible going into a negotiation. Be aware of assumptions and biases, which often become self-fulfilling.

Create Your First Offer

Before you walk into the room, have your first offer ready to go. This will be in the range of your best-case scenario. Then decide ahead of time what you're going to be willing to give up. This helps you control the process. Make sure you are asking for much more than what you are going to be willing to settle for.

Remember that people have to sort of be "beaten up" by the negotiation process before they'll come to a resolution sometimes. There are so many times that I have seen people end up at the exact same point as where one party had offered to resolve the matter at the outset. Oftentimes, until they've been tossed about in the negotiation boat and gotten seasick a few times, they still have grandiose ideas about how much they are going to get or what they think is a "fair" settlement.

So by having your first offer ready and then deciding ahead of time what you're going to be willing to part with or put another way, what the minimum is that you can live with, you will feel more in control of the process as it starts to unfold.

Figuring Out What to Ask For

People who go into a negotiation having done their research feel a sense of confidence and empowerment because they have the market information to support their position. So depending upon what it is that you are negotiating for, have an understanding of whether or not you will need to move from your position, or what they will have to do to move from theirs.

It's also important to go into a negotiation with an idea of what you're willing to accept if your first offer doesn't fly. If you decide before the negotiation what you're willing to accept (and what you're *not* willing to accept), you're less likely to make a rash decision on the fly or get talked into something and regret it later.

Make an Offer While You Ask

No matter what you're negotiating, you will always offer something of value while you are asking for something in return. The other side will want to feel that they are getting value, so if you want to get whatever it is that you are asking for, it is better to plan in advance what you are willing to give to the other side in return.

This comes back to the core message that every human wants to know that he or she matters and in a negotiation, that feeling of personal value is measured directly by the amount of value received in the transaction. Psychologically, the other side will immediately feel that you are recognizing their value, which will satisfy their own need. Once their needs are fulfilled, they will be more likely to feel at ease enough to want to give you something in return. This is sometimes referred to as the Law of Reciprocity.

Think of this in any business transaction. When companies are marketing to potential consumers, best practices dictate that you provide value first then go in for the ask. In negotiation, you always want to demonstrate that you are providing value to the other side, either prior to or contemporaneously with your ask.

There is another reason to do this. By providing value contemporaneously with the ask, you can use the value you are giving as leverage. This sounds a bit tricky but it is really simple. In other words, as you present the offer, you are asking for what you want in return but you are building in a sense of urgency. You are implying or perhaps stating directly, that what you are offering might not be available should they not decide to "play ball" with you right now.

This works for any kind of negotiating. For example, even if you're negotiating your cellular telephone bill, you can begin the conversation right off the bat by saying, "I'd be willing to sign another 2-year contract if you can lower my monthly bill to…"

Here, you're offering to be a long-term customer in exchange for what you want. You are also potentially threatening to defect over to a competitor.

Ask yourself: What do I have that would be of value to the other side?

Then: Create an offer which incorporates that value, match up that value to solve their pain points.

Once you have done all of this, you are ready to present.

Next up? Time to decide when and where the negotiation should take place.

Your Turf or Mine? Or Somewhere In Between?
Just as important as the timing, is choosing a venue that is appropriate. Should it be the other person's home base or yours? Or a neutral place that neither of you have ties to? There are definitely pros and cons for all three.

Everyone has heard the term "home field advantage" in relation to sports. This phrase was coined because not only do teams feel more comfortable in their hometown venues but they also are buoyed psychologically by their fans cheering them on and they are also used to the weather in their hometowns. All of this leads to more wins at home than when they are away. In fact, for example, the NCAA record for number of wins in a row is held by the University of Miami. Miami won 58 straight games at the Orange Bowl between 1985 and 1994. Almost ten years of straight wins playing on their home turf.

Does the home field advantage apply to negotiations? Two researchers decided to look into whether the "home field" advantage translates to other areas in life. In other words, is it to a person's advantage to be in an environment that is considered to be his or her own rather than the other person's? Behavioral scientists, Graham Brown and Markus Baer, looked specifically at the potential advantage for having the home turf in business. In order to perform the study, they asked pairs of individuals to assume the roles of purchaser and supplier. They asked them to role play a negotiation on the price of a fictional supply of something, with the very regular conversation being that the purchaser wanted to pay as little as possible and the supplier wanted the highest possible price for the supply.

In order to give one of the parties the "home advantage" they gave that person the option of personalizing the area in which the negotiations would take place. In other words, that person would be able to put his or her name on the outside of the office, would be able to choose which seat he or she sat in, and was given latitude to decorate the walls in whatever manner they wanted, and they even would give the home field person the keys to the offices.

The other side was not given the same circumstances. While the "home" person was decorating and personalizing the office, the other side was put in a place that was clearly described as temporary and for visitors. They knew that they were visiting the other person's offices. They were then brought into the "home" side's offices when the negotiations were actually about to begin.

Surprisingly, even though all of the above was totally contrived – meaning obviously both sides knew that neither actually had the "home" advantage – the party with the "home" advantage consistently outperformed the "visitor" side across the board. This was the case regardless of whether the person was playing the role of the purchaser or the role of the supplier.

Clearly there is something to the "home" advantage even outside the sports arena. But why? Obviously, weather shouldn't be an issue indoors and clearly there aren't generally crowds of fans cheering on a person sitting in an office. It all comes down to psychological factors. Once again, if you feel confident then you will perform better. It is in your home base that you know you matter and have value so you feel more powerful.

This means that it might be better to have the negotiations take place on your turf. But the flip side to this is that it means the other person is not as comfortable. This could potentially work against you. If the other side is uncomfortable then they could be more on edge, more defensive and more guarded. Meaning that they may be less apt to be agreeable and give in to what you want.

There also are non-verbal messages that are sent by agreeing to use the person's place. One is the message that you are confident. It sends a message that says "I know who I am and I feel strongly about the power of my position. In fact, I feel so comfortable that I don't mind coming to your place." You're communicating the message that you are not afraid of the conversation. You're also giving the other side the feeling that you respect them or even that you are going to be willing to listen to what they have to say.

There is another, much more oblique advantage to going to the other side's turf. That is that you will gather information about the person. If you haven't been in their teepee before, even if you don't end up having a final resolution, it could end up being a fantastic opportunity to sleuth. Take the time to observe photos on the wall or desk, or how the office is decorated. You will get a view into the person, what's important to him or her and maybe even what's driving or incentivizing that person. All very valuable information.

A neutral place is also an option. This choice also comes with its pros and cons. It may be perfect not to give either side the home field advantage but then you don't realize any of the benefits that using your turf or theirs might give you. If you do choose a neutral place, and that place is somewhere in the public such as a coffee place or a restaurant, be aware of a few things.

You will want to be certain that the time and place of the meeting is protected from outside interruptions. This is especially true if the subject of the conversation means a lot to you. You won't want people coming in and interrupting. This is why I personally don't love restaurants for certain conversations. It never fails that you are mid-sentence of something super heartfelt or you're expressing an incredible thought when suddenly you are interrupted with, "How are you enjoying the steak?" It totally interrupts the flow. You also don't want ringing telephones or texting. Put your phone away and leave it put away until the conversation is over. Depending upon who you're talking to, you may want to ask the other person to do the same. Obviously if it your boss or somebody superior to you then you might not be able to ask this of the other person.

When Shall We Meet?

Years ago, I was in the middle of a five-day custody trial, during which time my paralegal was working long hours also. The amount of preparation that goes into trials is huge and takes a tremendous amount of time leading up to and during the trial. Even after you've been in trial all day, you end up using the evenings to do additional legal research, update exhibits and hone your arguments. So on the third day of trial, while I am listening to my client being cross-examined by the opposing counsel, I received a text message from my paralegal that says, "*We need to talk about my overtime compensation.*" Um. Excuse me? You can only imagine my thoughts about negotiating her overtime pay at that moment.

After the trial was over and I was back to working in my office as usual, I asked her to meet with me to discuss, not only her request but also the way in which she requested it. I told her that if she really wanted something, which obviously in this case she did, that she should make sure that the person she wants something from actually is ready to hear what she has to say. I would even take that a step further and say make sure the person is in the mood to give you what you want.

Those of us who have children know this principle very well. My 16-year-old daughter will decide she wants something and then ask for it 100 times within an hour and even start gathering all sorts of arguments as to why I should give in to whatever the request is. A sample conversation:

Daughter: *Can I go to Coachella with my friends next year?*

Me: *I am in the middle of something right now. We can discuss that later. That's something we will have to talk about because there are many factors that need to be considered.*

Daughter: *All of my friends are going, and we would need to buy tickets way in advance. Everyone else's parents are letting them go.*

Me: *I told you I'm in the middle of something and we'd talk about it later.*

Daughter: *But so and so needs to know and plus I am mature enough and don't be the only parent who doesn't say yes.*

Now exasperated me: *I told you we'd talk about it – so if you need an answer now, the answer is NO.*

Does this sound familiar? There are really two times that the timing is going to be important here. The first is the actual asking for the meeting. The second is the time and place of the meeting itself. For both, you will want to be sure that the other person is in a place to hear what you are saying.

For the first part, where you are simply asking for the meeting, the timing is a bit less critical. You can perhaps email the person so that they can take a look at the email whenever they have the time to do so. Then the way you ask for the meeting will also be important. Leave off any tone of accusation, anger or judgment. A simple request without emotion or fighting words will be perfect. Let the other person know the subject of the meeting. Using my paralegal's example above, she could have sent an email that stated something like this:

"I know you are in trial right now, so this is not something that needs your attention until that is over, but after trial, I'd like to find a time that is convenient for both of us to discuss my overtime compensation."

That communication would have been fine but an even better one would be to have waited until after the trial was over. It was only two more days. Then she would have been able to write something much more positive, which would have motivated me to actually want to speak to her and give her what she wanted. Here is an example of how that would have looked:

"I know you're glad the trial is over. I am hoping for the best possible outcome for our client and it means a lot to me that I was

able to be a part of the trial team. I'd like to meet with you at a mutually convenient time to discuss the nature and computation of my overtime compensation. I wanted to wait until after the trial to approach you because I know how stressful trial can be. Should I go ahead and put some time on your calendar for us to talk? Or would you prefer to send me some potential dates/times that will work for you? Thanks so much for your consideration."

Had I gotten that email, I would have immediately responded that she could go ahead and find some time on my calendar and make the meeting happen. I would have been motivated to want to give her more not only because she was already laying the foundation of demonstrating her value, she also would have been acknowledging that she saw what was going on for me and that she was being considerate of that.

Your negotiation conversation is too important. Plan it correctly. Make sure the person with whom you need to speak is open to setting the meeting when you approach him or her about having a meeting initially, then be sure that when it is scheduled, it is scheduled for a time and place where you both will feel heard.

In order for both sides to feel like they matter, both sides will want to be able to speak and feel valued, so timing the conversation properly will be an important step toward winning what you want.

EXERCISES

1. What areas will I have to research in order to be prepared?
   Look back at the list included in the chapter to see if any of
   those items might apply.

   _____

   _____

   _____

   _____

   _____

   _____

2. Where will I have to look to find the information?

   _____

   _____

   _____

   _____

   _____

3. What will the other side's positions likely be?

   _____

   _____

   _____

   _____

   _____

4. What do I need to know about the other party? What research can I do?

_____

_____

_____

_____

_____

_____

5. What is motivating the other side?

_____

_____

_____

_____

_____

6. What are my best and worst case scenarios in this negotiation?

_____

_____

_____

_____

_____

7. What are my risks?

_____

_____

_____

_____

_____

_____

8. What are each of the separate issues that I will be discussing?

_____

_____

_____

_____

_____

9. What is my leverage that I either already have or can create? What are the other side's "pain points"?

_____

_____

_____

_____

_____

10. What will be my first offer?

_____

_____

_____

_____

_____

11. What value can I offer while I am asking for what I want?

_____

_____

_____

_____

_____

_____

12. Where should the negotiations take place? And why is that the optimum location?

_____

_____

_____

_____

_____

13. When should I ask for the meeting? Why is that a good time to ask?

_____

_____

_____

_____

_____

14. When should the meeting actually take place? Why is that a good time for the meeting?

_____

_____

_____

_____

_____

_____

Chapter 4 – Dress to a "T" – Then Use Those Power Words and Body Language

Never underestimate the power of a good outfit on a bad day.
~Unknown

TAKEAWAYS FROM THIS CHAPTER:

- Dressing in a way that makes you feel confident and powerful has a psychological impact and will take you another step toward getting what you want.
- Colors have a subliminal effect on people, so you'll want to be sure to select the color that you wear carefully
- You can use body language to exude power and build rapport
- By reading the other person's body language, you'll be able to adjust your presentation to ensure that you are maintaining the optimum rapport

Dress for Success

At first blush, this might seem like the fluff part of this book but there is quite an impressive body of research that proves that what you wear has a marked impact on your psyche, your poise and your presentation. The idea here is to dress in something that makes you feel confident and powerful for the negotiation. You might want to feel as if you look hot by wearing the power suit or red dress. You'll want to put on the lipstick or do the hair.

The New York Times did a study on the nexus between the clothes we wear and their impact on our psyche. They found that if a person wore a white coat they believed belonged to a doctor, then their attention increased sharply, but if they wore a white coat (same coat) they believed belonged to a painter, then there was no improvement. Scientists have come up with a fancy schmancy name to go with this phenomenon – it's called "*enclothed cognition*" – meaning that what you wear has an impact on how you think.

These findings are part of a larger area of psychology called embodied cognition, which stands for the proposition that we not only think with our brains, but our bodies participate in that process as well. Our physical experiences, including the clothes we wear, influence our thoughts. There are several examples, not necessarily clothing related that demonstrate this concept. When one washes his or her hands, one can associate that with being pure or ethically better than others. If one carries a certain type of briefcase or purse, one might feel more important.

The flip side of how you feel in the clothes is how others will *perceive* you. Studies have shown that women who dressed in more masculine attire had increased chances of being hired. Furthermore, people who dressed more professionally were perceived as smarter than those who did not.

In the study cited by the New York Times, people were given cognitive tests while wearing the doctors' coats and then while wearing regular street clothes. Overwhelmingly the groups performed better when they thought they were wearing the doctors' white coats. Your brain must associate that type, brand or kind of clothing with the emotion or trait that you want to exude. So if you associate being sexy while wearing lingerie then you'll exude raw sex appeal. If you associate Prada shoes with being fashionable, then you'll have an extra spring in your step while wearing them.

Dr. Karen Pine, in her book, *Mind What You Wear: The Psychology of Fashion*, states that what you're wearing has an impact, not only on your confidence, but also on your self-esteem. She asserts that something as simple as wearing a superhero T-shirt can make a person feel better about themselves.

Kia, the car manufacturer, did a study on what makes men and women feel more confident. While the results included things unrelated to clothing and appearance (i.e. a sunny day, being praised, perfume/after-shave), the lists did include other interesting revelations. For women, freshly shaved legs, a glowing tan, lipstick and a new haircut made a difference.

For men, being clean shaven, having freshly brushed teeth and wearing a new suit, was found to be just the confidence medicine needed to score that new job (or maybe even a new girl!).

Deep down, we didn't need these studies to state the obvious. Would "Wonder Woman" seem as powerful if she were wearing sweatpants and an old T-shirt? Would Russell Crowe have seemed as strong and mighty in "*The Gladiator*" had he been wearing a pink bunny costume instead of the full armor?

The clothes you are wearing invade your psychological processes and change your brain/body chemistry. So shave, put on the after-shave/cologne, get a haircut, put on the clothes that fit well and in which you feel strong, powerful and confident.

Color Me Powerful

Let me ask you a question: if I asked you what color is a power suit for a woman, what would be your answer?

Would it be ballerina pink? How about pastel green? No. No, it would not. Your answer would be red, am I right?

What are power colors for a man's suit? Beige? Seersucker blue pinstripe? Again, absolutely not. Your answer here would be navy or black, but that red would sneak back in again, but this time in the form of a tie. How often do we see powerful businessmen or male entrepreneurs wearing that navy suit with a red tie? It is a subliminal message to signal that this person is powerful.

Millions of dollars have been spent in industries across the board, from healthcare to fashion, and from financial planning to ecology, on what effect colors have on us humans. The impact is psychological, conscious, subconscious, emotional and physiological. In negotiations, colors make just as much of a difference. Here are some common colors, what they mean and what impact they have on negotiations:

Red: Red is often associated with intense emotions such as love, anger, passion, power and desire. It also signals danger and can be associated with violence. Fire engines and ambulances are red. So is blood. There is the Red Cross and the "Red Light" district. Even expressions using the word "red" are emotionally intense. "In the red" means you are spending more money than you have. There are "red flags", "red hot", "beet red" and "blood red." Considering all of that, it may be fairly obvious that in negotiations, red is not a color to wear if your plan is to actually get to a resolution. This is not a color of trust or safety. It can definitely be a power color so if your only goal is to intimidate then red might be the color for you. If your goal is to get the other person to resolve the issues, then it is not the optimum color.

Black: Closely related to red is the color black. Like red, black is a color of intensity. While it can mean power, strength, authority and formality, it also connotes death, evil, and negativity. Darth Vader wore all black. Certain psychologists have said that wearing all black day after day can even affect your own mood and even can cause depression and mood swings. While black can also mean sophistication and elegance, it is also associated with mourning, and can be even more sinister; gangs are often seen wearing all black. There is also a gender difference with black. So for negotiations, a man wearing all black might be perceived as sending a message of caution or to stay back, whereas with women, the message transmitted may be one of composure and poise. It is still not the ideal color for negotiations however, for either (or any) gender.

Orange: While orange is similar in hue to red, it is its own animal. Orange has aspects of yellow, which is warmer and more inviting. There is an energy to orange that causes a feeling a lightness, happiness and fun. The sun is orange, and orange juice is considered a morning pick me up. People who wear orange are viewed as more sociable, more friendly and more approachable. Orange is a safe color to wear in negotiations and does make a positive statement.

Green: Green is one of the natural colors that appears on the planet and so is viewed positively. It is often associated with healthy food, environmentally friendly products, conservation, as well as life, renewal, nature and energy. Green is also the color of money, which often is a positive connotation for people, so they think of green as meaning abundance, growth, luck and even balance. When people see others wearing the color of green, they feel a sense of calm, relaxation and soothing. Green can also bring a sense of hope, health, compassion and harmony.

Thus, green is a good color for negotiation. A couple of caveats however, olive green is associated with the army or illness, so that shade is not as desirable, and further, some psychologists say that too much green can even cause lethargy and placidity. Overall, however, green is a positive color for negotiations, especially jade or emerald greens.

White: In contrast to red or black, white means purity, innocence, light, cleanliness and goodness. It is the color we often see God or angels wearing and the color of a lot of soaps. We see doctors wearing white coats, as do brides, laboratory scientists and good guys. It's the color of snow and the color of the surrender flag. White can also mean new beginnings, wholeness, cleansing and renewal. Because of all of these meanings, when people are wearing white, the effect on the mind and body can be one of a feeling a clarity, and the encouragement of exorcising old negative thoughts and emotions, which will allow for positivity to flow. Therefore, white is a positive color to wear during a negotiation.

Purple: Purple is often associated with royalty, power, nobility, passion, fulfillment and luxury. Maybe that's why Prince liked purple so much. Purple often occurs naturally as well, as some of the most beautiful flowers are purple; lilacs, lavender, orchids and violets. These are some of the most beloved flowers and are considered to be precious, desirable and delicate. Purple is also associated with spirituality and is used with depicting astrology, third eyes and auras. Purple is a color of trust and therefore makes a great color for a negotiation.

Yellow: Yellow is bright, airy and light. Much like orange, but even without that intense red mixed in, yellow is friendship, love and safety. It also means freshness, optimism, clarity and happiness. Remember the old round smiley face. What color was that again? Oh right. YELLOW! It was also the color of ribbon used when people had loved ones at war, and they were praying and hoping for their safe return. (Cue the old song "Tie a Yellow Ribbon Round the Ole Oak Tree" by Tony Orlando and Dawn). While all this sounds lovely, yellow is also the color that signifies being a coward, fearful or "yellow." It can be perceived as weak and so it's a wonderful color for a Buddhist monk but not necessarily an optimum color for negotiating.

Blue: You often see blue in ads for financial advisors and lawyers. Doctors' scrubs are also blue. Think that's an accident? Yeah, NO! Blue is a color of trust, hope and optimism. It's the most prevalent color on the planet and is the color of water, the element that makes up 60% of us. Blue also connotes peace, trust, loyalty, stability, faith, the sky, confidence, heaven and intelligence. The color blue has positive effects on the mind and the body. We often see news anchors wearing blue, and it is also the color that is most often worn in job interviews. To be clear, when we are referencing blue here, it is usually a navy blue or a royal blue, not a neon or electric blue. Those colors cause more agitation and can do more harm than good in a negotiation.

While blue can also mean depressed or sad, it mostly brings a positive response and thus, blue is the winner of the color war when choosing something to wear for your big day.

To summarize the above, the best color choices to wear for a successful negotiation would be blue, green or purple, followed by orange and white. Probably best to avoid red, black or yellow in this instance. Save those colors for when they will serve you best. Figure how you feel and choose to wear a color that's going to make you want to slay the day.

Body Language – You Say More Than You Think

I have a confession to make. I had been doing negotiations for years, and then speaking about negotiation for years before I had the "aha" moment that body language is a huge part of the negotiation process. I had been invited to be a presenter at Campowerment, a camp created by a friend of mine which empowers and transforms lives. I presented on negotiation and there was another presenter there that weekend, who was presenting on body language. As I listened to her speak, the lightbulbs started going off in my brain that body language is a huge part of how we communicate to each other, even more so than the words that are actually coming out of our mouths.

That other speaker was a woman named Janine Driver, a *New York Times* bestselling author of two books, including *You Say More Than You Think*, and *You Can't Lie to Me*, and who also speaks all over the country on body language skills. After meeting her that weekend, she invited me to attend one of her weekend seminars in Washington D.C. and we co-facilitated a presentation on negotiation. Some of what I incorporate here I learned from her and from her resources and some is from other resources.

The one thing to be aware of about body language before we get into all the different indicators is that every single person has a baseline of body language also. So while all the following points are helpful, remember to just use them as a general guide. If you were really reading people the way they do for the FBI and other criminal investigations, you would want to make sure you were familiar with a person's regular ticks and tocks.

Building Rapport

When you first walk into that room, you are going to want to set the stage. Studies show that people make snap decisions about people within the first 30 seconds. This includes people that you know by the way. Have you ever seen your teenager come into the room with a big scowl and you immediately cringe because you know what's coming? Or do you have one of those friends who always greets you with that big, warm smile and your mood is immediately lifted the moment they are in your presence? I actually have seen a social media meme which says something like, "be the energy that shifts the room when you walk in."

Even if you think the other person doesn't like you, or thinks less of you, or you don't have positive feelings about the other person, make a deliberate decision before you even walk into the room that whatever the energy is that's going on, you are going to shift it to a higher level.

Next, there are a few rapport building tricks that you can also implement that will help you build that rapport immediately:

1. *Smile and shake the other person's hand.* This is great advice no matter what but here's the thing. You want your energy to be high, confident, and pumped. For those of you who are fans of the old television show *"The Office,"* remember how Dwight Schrute used to sit in his car before a big sales meeting and listen to loud rock music and pump his fists. Great stuff. He was raising his energy. Boxers do the same thing. Before they go into the ring, they've got their robes on, mouthguard in, they are jumping up and down and then they are ready to head into the ring. Pep rallies are another example. All of this is done so that by the time you walk into that room you are walking in with a presence. Think Meryl Streep in *"The Devil Wears Prada."*

   When you go to shake that person's hand, you are going to do so with unflappable confidence. If the other person is someone who you don't necessarily have a good relationship with, do it anyway. This will throw them off their game. They are going to expect you to ignore them or have an attitude. By smiling and immediately extending your hand, you are nonverbally communicating to that person that you are completely nonplussed by them or by this interaction.

While you are smiling and shaking the other person's hand, you should also say their name.

"Good morning, Susie. Good to see you today."

Or even just:

"Good afternoon, Joe. Thanks for agreeing to meet with me today. I appreciate your taking the time."

People like the sound of their own name. Why? Because it shows that you are seeing them, acknowledging them, showing them that they matter to you. Just that small detail will make a big difference in people's moods. Some body language experts actually suggest saying a person's name twice within the first 15 minutes of interaction, to get even more cooperation from them.

There is an underlying thing that's going on here too. You are telling the person that they matter, have value, and *you know it*! That will communicate to the other person a subliminal message that they too, should know that you matter and see your value. Remember, people will think what you tell them to think.

2. *Read Their Body Language and Mirror.* There is a technique in interacting with people called mirroring or mimicking. What that means is to sort of subconsciously take on the characteristics of the way the other person speaks or

interacts. So if a person is very formal, then you would also tend to be more formal. If the other person is sort of loud, curses and laughs a lot, then you would raise your vibrational frequency to match that.

Remember those mirror neurons we discussed in Chapter 2? When we are mirroring other's body language and way of speaking, we often are doing it without even realizing it. When my youngest daughter was little, we took her to visit some of my mother-in-law's family in Kentucky. My daughter was probably about 7 years old at the time. By the time, we were pulling out of the family's driveway, my daughter was talking with a stronger southern drawl than the people who were actually from Kentucky had! So funny. My husband and I asked her why she was talking like that and she responded, "Well, I'm tryin' to tawlk normal but Ah just cain't!"

We all feel more comfortable when we are around people that we think are like us, so by putting the other side at ease and tactically thinking that you are more like them, they will be more apt to do what you want them to do. Now, there is a bit of a caveat to this methodology. You definitely want to be sure that the other side doesn't see you copying them. In other words, don't make it look ridiculous like they cross their legs, then you cross your legs. Use this technique in sort of a covert way that appears natural.

3. *Let Them Talk First.* I did divorce negotiations for years and one of the things that I often did was let the other side go first. It shows you are respecting them and being nice, and demonstrates that you want to hear what they have to say. There also is another side to this. A tactical side.

   For one thing, you are giving the other side the floor first. You can ask open ended questions or just let them talk. In my initial client meetings with divorcing clients, before I even enter into the nuts and bolts of divorce law or procedure, I just let people talk. They have so much that they need to get off their chests. They often have been thinking about what they are going to discuss for so long and just giving them the chance to open up and share their thoughts and feelings will immediate set the stage that you are valuing what they have to say, causing them to be disarmed.

   You will also learn quite a lot about what their thinking is, what their positions are and why, just by letting them have time to share. Life coaches are also trained to just let people share and talk, as are therapists. This will provide insight into what is incentivizing them, what's motivating them, and most importantly, what it is they want from you which will make them feel that they matter to you, that you are seeing their value and what you need to do to validate that.

4. *Listen Actively.* There are lots of passive aggressive ways to not listen to a person. Looking at your phone, looking

away, appearing distracted are all examples of not listening attentively. When you do engage in those types of behaviors, the other person certainly does not feel heard and doesn't feel as if they matter. Now, you might have nothing but disdain for the other person, but even with those deep-seated feelings of negativity, there is something you want from that person. Otherwise why would you be bothering to have the conversation?

The ways that people feel heard and seen are nodding your head as they speak, saying "yes" or "uh huh", looking into their eyes and giving them your rapt attention as they state their positions. Another way to listen actively is to paraphrase back what they have said. That would sound something like this.

"So, what I am hearing you say is that you feel undervalued at this company because you are not being compensated in the manner you feel is commensurate with your skills."

5. *Be Respectful. Always.* One of my favorite things to say is that you can disagree without being disagreeable. I used to have to say that to some opposing counsel. In fact, one time, I had a newer lawyer on the other side. I have found over the years that younger lawyers, or lawyers who aren't really sure about what they are doing, tend to try to compensate for their lack of knowledge by being overly aggressive. This can

sometimes become personal. In this particular case, during the deposition of my client, who happened to be the wife, the opposing counsel was just absolutely and stunningly disrespectful. He asked her about plastic surgery she had had done, made snide remarks that were audible about how awful it looked, and snickered openly at some of her answers.

The first thing I did was to state on the record, meaning the court reporter typed it down, that he was being unprofessional and that if he continued with this approach, I would report him for ethical violations.

The second thing I did was to pull him aside, without his client or my client present, and said to him, "You know, you and I are not getting divorced here. You don't need to act like this. We are colleagues and we are going to see each other again." He actually sheepishly responded to me that his client felt as if he wasn't being tough enough so that he believed he needed to display how tough he was in front of him. I gave him credit for being honest in that way but I was still disgusted at his behavior.

No matter what the circumstances are, if you value yourself, you will be respectful.

Remember, the way people treat other people is a reflection of how they feel about themselves; NOT a reflection of how they feel about you. People who feel good about themselves, who are secure in their value, will always treat others with respect. They know it doesn't take away from their own value to treat others with dignity. The impact is greater than just treating the other person with respect. The other person will now not only be more willing to comply with your requests, but they also will respect you more.

Side note: Do not confuse fear with respect. Some people try to garner what they think is respect by throwing their power around and treating everyone cruelly. That just breeds contempt in people. They might do what you want them to, but they won't respect you and it won't be for long.

6. *The Belly Button Rule*: This rule states that where your little naval is facing is where your attention lies. This means you could be facing a person but have your naval be facing the door, which means guess what? You're thinking about how to get outta there! This is something which we all have a subconscious knowledge about, so we know if someone's torso is faced toward us that we have that person's attention.

7. *Ask Open Ended Questions:* Asking open-ended questions will help you to not only build rapport but also gather information about what the other side's positions and motivations are. When they are telling you their position or advancing their arguments, you will respond with questions such as "Tell me more about that" or "What makes your feel that way?" or "How did you come to that conclusion?" Be

sure to stay away from "Why" questions as those put people on the defensive.

Power Body Language Moves

When you walk into that room with that air of confidence, knowing your value, that will already send a message. There are also a few other things that you can easily incorporate into the way you present yourself which will also help you to appear more powerful. The great thing about these body language moves is that you can do them easily. You know the old "fake it till you make it" adage? This is great way to fake it even if you aren't feeling super confident:

1. *Curb Your Enthusiasm*: While you want to smile, extend your hand and say hello, do not in any way appear eager to resolve the issue. This will give away some of your leverage and you definitely want to keep that until you are strategically ready to use it.

2. *Power Stances*: Research done by Columbia and Harvard business schools show that standing in a powerful position, creates the illusion of power. Both feet approximately shoulder width apart, head up, chin forward, and hands can either be open at your sides, or arms can be crossed.

   The arms being crossed has been misconceived over the years. Many people associate it with feeling insecure and others with power. But in general, it conveys power and confidence. That's why so often you see ads for lawyers or finance people in suits with their arms crossed.

Just don't keep your hands in your pockets and slouch your shoulders down. That will convey that you are anxious or worried in some way. It will definitely not communicate that you are valuable and confident. Remember, you want the other side to see you, to know you have meaning and value.

In her book, *Presence*, Amy Cuddy discusses whether body language is derived from nature or nurture. She says that research shows that there are certain expressions and body language which are universal. For example, if we feel the emotion of disgust, regardless of where you are from in the world, you turn up your nose, your lips go up, our eyes widen and maybe even roll, and our mouths open slightly.

Amy Cuddy goes on to explain how pride is a feeling that is expressed throughout the body. Several years ago, researchers showed pictures to graduate students of people standing. The people were standing in "an expanded and upright posture, head tilted slightly upward (about 20 degrees), a small smile, and arms either akimbo with hands on the hips or raised above the head with hands in fists." They were asked how they would describe the people in the photos. The majority of the students used adjectives to describe that photos such as *proud, triumphant, self-confident*.

You can also lean back in your chair and put your hands behind your head down next to your neck. You often see business guys in movies who assume that position and even put their feet up on the desk. I don't recommend the feet on the desk. It might come across as rude and even arrogant. But just look at how doing one or two things that make someone appear cocky and/or over-confident.

3. *Steepling*. You often see doctors, politicians and even presidents doing this. This is where you take both your hands and put them together so that just your fingertips are touching and forming a little steeple. Do you remember anyone doing this? You instantly look smarter and as if you know what you're doing.

4. *Chin Grab*. This is again a very easy move that you can just nonchalantly throw in when no one is expecting it. You simply just take your chin between your thumb and your fingers and you just hold your chin loosely. Think of the economist with the bow tie, slowly stroking the beard on his chin while he imparts his knowledge of where interest rates are going and why.

   At Janine Driver's workshop on body language, she showed a picture of the previous CEO of Pepsi grabbing her chin during one of her interviews. There are also pictures of Janine herself grabbing her chin in publicity shots. You don't want to grab it and hold onto like you are holding on for dear life or trying to steady yourself. You are just sort of loosely touching it while you are intently listening and contemplating what the other person is saying, or while you are gracing the room with your own pearls of wisdom.

5. *Arm Drape.* The arm drape is something I've actually done for years just because it seemed more comfortable to me. Who knew that it was actually a power move? This is simply when you are sitting in a chair, you take your elbow and lift to rest on the back of the chair. It works best obviously if you are in a chair large enough and with a low enough back. It allows you once again to appear open. When you appear open, then you look as if you aren't afraid, and you are ready to address anything that is said to you.

6. *Hands on Hips.* This one is one that I offer cautiously. The power move is both hands on your hips. Not just one. If a person only has one hand on one hip, then the message is actually completely different. It conveys maybe anger, or at the very least a sassiness. This is the pose that you see the teenagers making in ads for Hollister or Abercrombie, or your very own precious child standing in your kitchen when you tell him or her that going out on Friday night is not happening. But very often on the red carpet, you will

see celebrities or models assuming this stance and they look open or confident.

Reading Other People's Body Language

In addition to the advice I offer above for you to implement, it is important that you can read the other person's body language too. Here are the essentials:

1. *The Shoulder Shrug.* If someone says something that makes perfect sense but then shrugs their shoulders while they are saying it, that is considered a communication that is actually disagreeing with the words that are coming out of their mouths. Here is an example:

   Q: "What is your relationship like with your team at work?"
   A: "It's pretty good." (while shoulder is shrugging).

   In the example above, you can see that without the shoulder shrug, you would have been more likely to believe that the person's relationship with his or her team at work actually is pretty good. With the shoulder shrug, you are not so sure.

   A great example of this can be seen in videos of people who are not necessarily telling the truth on television interviews. In one such case, when one of the boys was interviewed about whether or not he had been touched inappropriately by Michael Jackson, he vehemently was denying it and saying how much he loved being at his house, when all the while his shoulder was bobbing up and down like a buoy in the ocean. Years later, he came out and admitted to the press that he was indeed not being truthful during that earlier interview.

In negotiation meetings with people, you will swear that you had an agreement with the other person, and then they almost immediately renege on what you thought was a deal. What you didn't see was that as they were agreeing, they might have been shrugging their shoulders.

2. *Self-Touching.* No. This isn't that. This is actually a form of self-soothing and it stems from when we were babies. We learned to pacify ourselves when we were stressed. So, if you see someone (or catch yourself!) doing something like rubbing your arm or leg, that might be a sign of anxiety or stress. You'll sometimes see people putting their hands in their pockets when they are nervous. Having their hands closer to them, almost as if they are wrapping themselves in a security blanket, makes them feel safer and more secure.

Touching their head and hair is also a telltale sign. For men, they tend to ventilate their hair from the top, almost as if they are combing it back from the forehead to the crown of their heads. Women, interestingly enough, come from the other side. They tend to go to the nape of the neck and ventilate upward into the back of their heads. These can also be signs that someone is lying, so be on the lookout for that!

121

3. *Shaking or Nodding Head.* Remember how nodding the head can help develop a rapport. There is another reason to be aware of what you are doing with your noggin. Sometimes people will say things that are not in harmony with what's going on with their heads. Similar to what's happening with the shoulder shrug, a person could be saying something that appears like agreement but shaking his or her head in the process. Again, if you aren't attuned to what's going on, you could feel blindsided down the road when the other person suddenly says that they no longer want to execute the contract to which you have agreed. Here is an example:

   You: *It was so great to meet you!*

   Other person: *It was (shaking head) so great to meet you too!*

   The other person is not feeling as if it was so great to meet you for whatever reason.

4. *Shifting Eyes.* If the other person has been attentive to you the entire conversation, but then you say something that causes them to suddenly shift their eyes, that could signal disagreement or perhaps that they are now lying. Either way, you are no longer in accord. Something has happened that has caused the other person to shift and they will tell you that they have shifted by darting their eyes or looking in a different direction.

5. *Upper Lip.* What happens when you don't like a food? Your lip goes right up. Lip up means disgust. This applies not only to disgust of food though. This also applies to disgust when you are having a conversation with someone. If you see the other person's lip start to curl up, then you are not on the same page.

   Another thing that happens with lips, if that someone can purse them. If you see a person's lip curl inward, so that you are no longer really seeing them. That is your signal that they are probably none too pleased. My German grandmother used to have a way of pursing her lips, and having her pursed lips make a little sound. You could actually hear it on the telephone. For example, if we called her, and she felt it had been too long since we had called her last, she would say "Well silence is golden. Certainly, where you're concerned," followed by pursed lips with little a little sucking sound so it could be heard through the phone line 100 miles away. There are numerous examples of this in the news when a celebrity is being grilled about some bad behavior they have engaged in and don't want to talk about; Lance Armstrong, John Edwards and Kobe Bryant are just a few.

6. *Facial Blocking or Hiding in Hair.* If a person doesn't want to be seen emotionally, they will try to hide themselves. While we all want to be seen and heard and feel as if we

have meaning, if we feel that we are going to be exposed or feel vulnerable, then the little child inside will want to run and hide. If we can't actually jump up and run out of the room and hide, then we will subconsciously look for ways to hide, like putting our hands to our face or letting our hair fall down around our face.

7. *Involuntary Responses.* When people get nervous or angry, our bodies start wanting to protect us. It might seem like our bodies are actually turning on us, but it is really that the epinephrine is kicks in and gets ready for the fight or flight. We all know how these look and feel. We start to sweat, not just in our armpits, which is bad enough, but often sweat will form little attractive beads on the line of our lips, or worse, on our foreheads.

The other fun thing that starts to happen is that our mouth can go dry and then we start swallowing more. We can also start breathing more deeply, or our hearts start to race. With all that extra blood flow, we can even get red in the face or go pale.

Sometimes, if we are nervous our hands start to shake. I remember watching my first boss as a lawyer. She was a world class attorney who had an impeccable reputation. As many years as she had been practicing, and as skilled as she was, she would still always get nervous in the courtroom. I vividly remember watching in disbelief as she would present a stellar argument to the judge, all the while gripping the counsel table like grim death.

Unfortunately, these are all involuntary responses. How we combat the involuntary responses is by putting ourselves in a position where we are less nervous, less unsure of ourselves, and less unprepared. You can actually control the physiological responses by implementing the methods in this book – doing 80% of the preparation ahead of time – knowing your own internal value, doing your research, preparing your arguments, anticipating what the other side's positions are going to be, being ready with responses, creating your leverage, and walking in with confidence and purpose.

8. *Nose Rubbing.* This one is also a tricky one. Because while our noses can start to tickle because of a physiological response that happens when we lie (perhaps the basis of the Pinocchio story?), we also touch our noses for lots of other reasons. Many people have allergies, or they might have a cold, or they might even just have a habit of touching their noses. This is one of those indicators that you might want to be aware and watch for while you are interacting with the other person.

Start practicing reading other people's body language now, so that when you are in a negotiation conversation, it is second nature to you. Once you understand it, then you will be able to either adjust your conversation, your strategy, and your tactics accordingly so that you can be sure you remain on the path to winning exactly what you want.

EXERCISES

1. What clothes do you have that make you feel confident and powerful when you put them on?

    _____

    _____

    _____

    _____

    _____

2. What colors do you think would be best to wear for the negotiation meeting? And why are you choosing those colors?

    _____

    _____

    _____

    _____

    _____

3. Of the rapport building tricks listed in this chapter, which ones do you plan to practice and then implement during your negotiation?

    _____

    _____

    _____

    _____

_____

_____

4. Of the list of power body language moves provided in this chapter, which ones will you practice and then implement into your negotiation style?

_____

_____

_____

_____

_____

5. How can you start practicing reading other people's body language now?

_____

_____

_____

_____

_____

Chapter 5 – "T" – Tackle the Hard Issues Second (or Start with Areas Where You Might Agree and Work Toward the More Contested Issues)

Facts are stubborn things; and whatever may be our wishes, our inclinations, or the dictates of our passions, they cannot alter the state of facts and evidence.

~John Adams

TAKEAWAYS FROM THIS CHAPTER:

- When you start your negotiation conversation, you will want to start with areas of agreement then work toward areas that are more likely to be inflammatory because you will create a feeling of trust, respect and the momentum of accomplishment

- Be careful not to collapse personal feelings with objective criteria

- Communicate your facts and positions in a manner that is brief, informative, friendly and firm.

Start with the Uncontested Facts

When I was in high school, I actually loved physics. It was one of my favorite classes. It probably helped that I had a teacher who believed in me (hint: made me feel that I mattered....), but I also just really loved how it all made logical sense. So when it comes to negotiating, it makes total sense to me to incorporate some of the laws of physics. Remember what laws are in science. They were once hypotheses that were then tested over and over and over again, until the scientists determined that there is never a deviation. They can rely on the fact that when applied, the outcome will be the same virtually every single time. No nonconformity.

In negotiation, you will also want to start with the facts. You will want to keep those facts present at all times. The reason you will want to do that is because facts make your arguments that much stronger. Just as John Adams stated in the above quote, whatever our wishes, inclinations or passions may be, we can't change facts. They aren't altered by perceptions. So in law, we learn to use facts to our advantage. We present the facts, data and research that support our positions. The more you present, the stronger your argument is. Even better, is when you can weave in facts, research and data that refute the other person's position.

Sticking with our strategy to rely on the laws of science to help us win the negotiation and get what we want, the second strategy is to start with areas of agreement and then work toward the contested issues. Sir Isaac Newton's very first law of motion is also sometimes referred to as the Law of Inertia or the Law of Motion. What that law states is that an object at rest stays at rest and an object in motion stays in motion with the same speed and in the same direction unless acted upon by an unbalanced force.

I have sat through the most highly emotional and hotly contested negotiations there are. If I had a $100 for every time a person told me they are certain their case won't settle because the other side is so unreasonable, I would definitely be Oprah's next-door neighbor by now. Here's the thing you really need to understand about negotiation. In the beginning, most people have high expectations. They think they are going to get everything that they want or that they deserve and even fantasize about what that will look like. But the reality is what I mentioned earlier. First, there are three sides to every story and second, no one is going to settle for their worst day.

So what you want to do, using the law of motion, is get the feeling of positivity and cooperation flowing along, then you can ride that wave all the way to resolution. The way to do that is to start with areas you think you can agree upon. How that might look when you are asking for a raise is this:

You: *"I think we can both agree that we want this company to grow and capture more of the market share in our industry."*

Your boss: *"Absolutely. We've been working hard toward that goal."*

You: *"I know we have. I'm so excited to be part of the expansion. I think we can also agree that we want to achieve the company's goals in the most cost efficient and timely manner possible."*

Your boss: *"Definitely."*

You: *"I also know that you have seen how dedicated I have been. My sales numbers this year are up 20% so far, I have brought in 5 new accounts, and have trained all the new employees."*

Your boss: *"We have really appreciated your efforts."*

You: *"I am grateful to be in a company that appreciates and rewards employees who are loyal to the company and committed to its growth. In that vein, I'd like to discuss increasing my compensation with the company."*

You see how by starting with areas of agreement *and* pulling in facts, you lead the boss directly to the conclusion that you want her to draw. You started off talking about the goals of the company and then demonstrated how important that is to you. You have shown that you understand the company's objectives and how you have helped the company achieve those objectives. There can be no other conclusion than that you are entitled to additional compensation.

Be Careful Not to Collapse Personal Feelings with Objective Criteria

A couple of years ago, I had a paralegal who was great at her job but also had an issue with paid time off. She was a single mom with two young children at home and felt that the three weeks of paid vacation that she received as part of her benefits was inadequate. Her reasoning was that she had young children and had to use her vacation for taking the children to the doctors or staying home with them if they were sick or off from school for example. In her world, that meant she had no extra time for vacation. We discussed it and explained to her that while we sympathized with her position, she had been given a generous amount of vacation time and also received paid days off when the firm was closed for holidays.

Unhappy with that response and rather than try to work within rules, she instead constantly searched for ways to "game" the system in an attempt to get more paid time off. She would "forget" to hand in her PTO request form. She would say she was running late and then come in a half a day later but not use that as PTO, and many other ways. She was quite creative, I must say.

So, one day, my law partner and I sat down with her and our Human Resources manager to discuss the matter with her. She started crying and launched into how devoted she was to the firm and how hard she works. She also pointed to how much time the law partners took off and how the lawyers made so much more money than she.

So, let's analyze what was really going on here? Here is a person who wanted to feel valued. She had created a big story as we do. Her story was that the whole system wasn't fair. That she wasn't paid enough, that she didn't have enough paid time off, and that in general, she was just not being appreciated. This is a great example of being guided by emotions rather than the facts. The facts were that she was a paralegal. She was earning the top pay for a paralegal in the area. She also was an employee. Employees do not get the same perks as owners. They also don't take the same risks and they are also not responsible for bringing in business and making sure payroll is met and that the rent is paid. Remember, her *external* value was being driven by the market for paralegals in that area at that size law firm.

But key here is that she was collapsing together things that shouldn't be mixed. In her mind, if we cared about her, if we saw her value, and if we appreciated her, then we would have allowed her to come and go as she pleased and we would have paid her as much as the law partners were making. This is an unreasonable request and doesn't comport with the objective criteria, which was that she was a paralegal. Our feelings about her as a person were separate from her position at the firm. What she was doing was collapsing her feelings of value with the objective criteria of what is standard for a paralegal, and an employee. One had nothing to do with the other.

The lesson here is this. Your value as a human being is your value as a human being and that is innate. Remember that your *internal* value is immoveable. You are whole and you matter. Your value in the world as a career person, is driven in some measure by objective criteria. In the above example, because we liked her as a person, and thought she did an overall great job when she was there, we did pay her at the top of the paralegal scale. But that didn't mean that to show her that we appreciated her and valued her, we would then pay her far *more* than she was worth as a paralegal. Be careful not to collapse your emotions with objective criteria.

Be Present to Your Presentation

"Just the facts, ma'am." I wasn't old enough to watch *Dragnet* on television when it was actually on. I did however catch it in reruns occasionally, and I remember that the main character, Joe Friday, would implore the females that he was interviewing to stick to "just the facts, ma'am, just the facts." All potential misogyny aside, there was some great wisdom there that we can remember when you present your position.

You will want to present your position in a way that is persuasive but sounds like you are just presenting facts. A little bit of dance but very doable. What you don't want to do is throw in little digs or sprinkle in your feelings about how life isn't fair to you or sounds argumentative. The more emotionally invested you are in the situation or the person, the more at risk you are for this to happen. So decide ahead of time, what you are going to say will be critical.

This is counterproductive behavior, because obviously you want something from the other person or you wouldn't be engaging in a negotiation. But sometimes we can't help ourselves.

I once was representing a former husband who was defending himself against a former wife who was suing him for more child support. My client had always paid the court ordered amount of child support on time and had even willingly paid for many other items for his son. As soon as we were in front of the mediator, the former wife had 100 different ways of describing the former husband, while she was also explaining her current job situation and what she thought the former husband was currently earning (earnings of the parties were the only relevant facts in this negotiation), and all of her descriptions came down to the same core message: that the former husband was a deadbeat dad. Now, the former husband was just irked and feeling as if he needed to defend himself to the mediator. This was not a good strategy on the former wife's part because now he definitely wasn't feeling motivated to do what she wanted him to do, which was to pay more child support.

What the former wife should have done instead is to stick to the facts. She could have presented what the law is for child support modification – that it can be modified if there has been a substantial change in circumstances of the parties' incomes –

and then proceed to present the current incomes of each of the parties along with new child support guidelines based upon the new incomes. Then the former husband would have been much more willing to have a conversation. He could have refuted the income numbers for himself and supported that argument with facts, or he could have used data to show why the child support guidelines figures were incorrect.

So in other words, to start with areas of agreement, the better way to have presented the information above, would have been to say something like this:

> *Here is a copy of our state's statute on modification of child support. It states that child support can be modified if, when the guidelines are run based on the current incomes of the parties, there is more than a 15% deviation in what the original court-ordered child support was, then a modification is warranted. We have run the guidelines based on the average of the last three months of paystubs for both of the parties and find that the new child support figure would be 18% higher than the current court-ordered child support, so therefore, under the law, modification is necessary.*

By sticking to the facts but using them in a persuasive manner, and starting with areas of agreement you can walk people right into coming to the conclusion that you want.

In family law, the author Bill Eddy has offered co-parents who are experiencing acrimony, an acronym for remembering how to communicate with each other. He says to use the BIFF method, meaning to keep all interactions Brief, Informative, Friendly and Firm. The BIFF method is also a perfect way to remember how to present your positions in any type of negotiations.

There is another very important reason to start with areas of agreement. This is especially important if you are working through several complicated issues. People like the feeling of accomplishment. Most people also want to be liked and want to be perceived as being "reasonable." If you can start with areas in which you think are going to be easier to resolve then that will set the tone for the rest of the conversation. Each person is feeling heard, feeling validated and feeling respected. That momentum will cause both parties to want to keep going. Then once you get to the harder issues, the more contested issues, both sides will be more apt to let go of positions they might have once held onto steadfastly. They will believe they can do that and still hold onto their own dignity, self-worth and feelings of value.

EXERCISES

1. What are the uncontested facts that you will both be able to agree upon?

   _____

   _____

   _____

   _____

   _____

2. Which of the facts that are uncontested will be the most optimum ones to your conversation?

   _____

   _____

   _____

   _____

   _____

3. What are the contested issues or the issues that may tend to become inflammatory?

   _____

   _____

   _____

   _____

   _____

4. What is the objective criteria that the person you will be negotiating with is going to be looking at?

_____

_____

_____

_____

_____

5. Are there any emotional issues that you will need to remember to separate out from the objective criteria?

_____

_____

_____

_____

6. What will be the best way to present your opening when you begin your negotiation? What exactly do you plan to say?

_____

_____

_____

_____

Chapter 6 – "E" – Keep Your Emotions in Check

Life is an ongoing process of choosing between safety (out of fear and need for defense) and risk (for the sake of progress and growth). Make the growth choice a dozen times a day.
~Abraham Maslow

TAKEAWAYS FROM THIS CHAPTER:

- By doing the prep work, inside out: M – A – T – T above, you will feel more in control and will be unflappable during the big conversation
- Learning to keep your emotions in check will ensure that you are unflappable, even if you are dealing with someone who is overly difficult or is much more powerful than you are
- Mastering the art of embedded commands will help you to get what you want and stay cool, calm and collected
- Scripts help you frame how you will ask for what you want; improvise when you have become a master of the facts and arguments

Second That Emotion

One of the first things young student teachers and young parents learn is that when you have lost control, children know they have you. It is the same thing in negotiation. Often people will say or do things that will push your buttons. This may be a tactic to deliberately unhinge you, or even to manipulate you. The natural reaction, especially if you feel as if you're being attacked, is to fight back and to defend yourself. You don't want to appear weak or allow someone to get the better of you, so you react. However, the minute you respond with losing your cool, or tears or anything that shows that the other side has been able to rattle you, you've now completely lost control of the situation.

There can be some differences in the way men approach negotiating versus the way women negotiate. Of course, this is a bit of a generalization and there are exceptions to the rule, but some observations about how the different genders negotiate may be useful in keeping in mind as you think about how to prepare for your conversation.

Men are single focused by nature. This can drive women crazy sometimes, but they really only have the ability to think about one thing at a time. This means that when they are at work, they are thinking about work. I heard a comedian do a bit on this once and he referred to a man's mind as a set of boxes. Men have a box for work, a box for their love relationship, a box for their hobby, and so forth. Each box can only be taken out one at a time. Another box is not even able to be checked out of the mind library unless the other boxes have been neatly put away. This means that men can completely shut off the emotional aspect of negotiating in a lot of ways– except sometimes they can let anger get the best of them – but in general they are much better at controlling their emotions.

Women brains are all hard wired into their emotions and those emotions are all connected to everything else. Women also have the ability to think about several things at once. It is sort of like a computer that has 50 tabs open at the same time, and then each of those tabs are connected to emotions. As an aside, this is why women generally have better memories than men. We remember how we felt about certain experiences. Remember how Maya Angelou once said that we don't necessarily remember what our teachers taught us, but we do remember how they made us feel? Because women generally are much more in touch with their emotions, they tend to remember things more readily.

In negotiations then, women tend to expect people to see the whole of them – the person who stood by the other's side – they expect loyalty and to be recognized for sacrifices, or they expect the other side to understand how they are feeling. This usually does not go very well for women for a variety of reasons. First, if they are negotiating with a man, not only does he not see the feelings, he doesn't even compute that he is supposed to be reading the feelings. He is simply thinking about the task at hand. This is especially true if the man has a lot of experience in negotiating. He knows he has a single focus, and that is to accomplish this particular deal and reach a particular outcome.

The woman on the other hand, not only wants to accomplish the deal and have a particular outcome but she also wants to feel good about it. She wants to feel that she has been validated, appreciated, seen, valued, and heard. While a man wants some of that too, it is not usually his primary goal. He does want to be respected and valued but that will be measured by him in the outcome.

For both genders, learning and understanding how the other side thinks and feels can go a long way. Taking the time to understand what drives each side will be critical. Then you can learn to communicate in a way that each side feels heard.

What if The Other Side is Overly Difficult or More Powerful?

In my law practice, I often have had clients, usually women, who have tried to convince me how difficult it will be to get anything out of the other side because of how "powerful" their husbands are. This perceived "power" makes the other side feel as if they are at a disadvantage. The other thing that seems to be much more prevalent nowadays is dealing with narcissists. Whether the other person actually is a narcissist in a clinical sense, or whether they are just completely difficult to deal with is really of no import. The result is the same. You are dealing with a personality that feels impossible.

Let me just tell you that most of the time, this has all been manipulated to make you feel that way. Remember, people will think what you tell them to think and if the other side wants you to think they are more powerful, that you should be worried, that they have an edge over you in some way, and you've bought into it? Then they have achieved their objective.

A great example of this was when a female client was interviewing me to potentially represent her in her divorce case. She had been a stay-at-home mother for probably 20 years and hadn't had any big career before that. Her husband was a wealth advisor who brought home about $3 Million in income a year, which had allowed them to live quite a nice lifestyle. They had their home in the city and their home right on the shore. The children attended posh private schools and they traveled around the world in first class style regularly.

I began to conduct the initial meeting in my usual way. She started by telling me what was going on – he had had an affair – she found the Victoria's Secret receipt in his car – she was heartbroken, angry, hurt and very scared. Scared that she was going to get nothing. Worried that he held all the cards. Nervous that he would outmaneuver her in the divorce. I gave her my "short crash course" in Florida family law, applied the law to her situation to give her the range of what she was looking at in all the areas (property division, alimony, custody, child support and attorneys' fees – see my first book, *Breaking Free: A Step by Step Guide to Achieving Emotional, Physical and*

Spiritual Freedom for more on that) and then went through the procedure of a divorce. That all assuaged her concern somewhat.

But then she turned to me and said, "*Rebecca, my husband is the type of guy that is going to run out and get the BEST divorce attorney in the area. Would you be ready for that?*"

My response? "*Well, he won't be able to do that.*"

"*Why not?*" she asked.

"*Because you already will have hired me.*" I stated with the voice of authority, but with a slight smile.

She smiled and took a breath, then said with a sigh of relief, "*Yup. You're the right one for me.*"

What happened there was all in HER thinking. We hadn't even spoken to the husband. But in our short interaction, she went from believing there was no way she could ever win against him, to feeling that she could. So, the first step in working with someone who you think is more powerful or extremely difficult is *believing that it is possible to get what you want despite those traits.*

Even if you haven't been manipulated to feel that way, and the other person is just incorrigible, there are ways of going around that and still getting the person to give you what you want, and even have them be okay with giving you what you want! It's all in the strategy. One of the best strategies you can use is to implement "embedded commands" into your delivery.

Embedded Commands

Embedded commands sound complicated, but they really aren't. They are pretty much exactly what they sound like. They are commands to another person that are "embedded" in the form of a question or a statement. It is actually a strategy taught when you learn Neurolinguistic Programming or NLP.

Many of us actually use this technique a lot without even realizing what we are doing. A good example of this might be something like:

> *"I know you love me and want the best for me, so I know you won't want to do something that you know is hurting me."*

You are basically telling the person either what to think or what you want them to do but burying it or rather, embedding it, into the form of a statement or a question. Sort of like a subliminal message, you are actually sending subconscious commands to the other person's brain.

While some people have called this form of speaking manipulative or even sneaky, really it is just a tool that you can keep in your toolkit, just like all of the rest of the tools you are learning here. Tools can be used for good or they can be used for bad, but the tools in and of themselves are not inherently good or bad.

You will however want to use them in a way that feels both authentic while also maintaining a feeling of respect for the other person. This technique has you weaving together what you want the other person to do and something that you think might be important or incentivizing to them.

One of the greatest examples of this is when Mr. Rogers was before Congress, asking for PBS funding for his television program for children. The year was 1969 and it was widely known that the senator in front of whom he would be appearing, was a tough nut to crack. Senator John Pastore was known for being gruff and impatient, a manner that he assumed when the mild-mannered former Presbyterian minister appeared in front of him that day in May. Incredibly it took just six minutes for Mr. Rogers to get Senator Pastore to come around, and by using his authentic approach and lots of embedded commands, he was able to procure $20 MILLION dollars in funding! Using an inflation rate of 5%, that would be more than $130 Million in today's dollars. Staggering! But definitely worth implementing a few embedded commands. So how did he do it? Here is the entire script. Can you find the embedded commands? Read it in its entirety, then we will go through how Mr. Rogers worked his magic on someone known to be difficult and who seemed to not only have more power, but all the power!

Senator Pastore: All right Rogers, you've got the floor.
Mr. Rogers: Senator Pastore, this is a philosophical statement and would take about ten minutes to read, so I'll not do that. One of the first things that a child

learns in a healthy family is trust, and I trust what you have said that you will read this. It›s very important to me. I care deeply about children.

Senator Pastore: Will it make you happy if I read it?

Mr. Rogers: I'd just like to talk about it, if it's alright. My first children's program was on WQED fifteen years ago, and its budget was $30. Now, with the help of the Sears-Roebuck Foundation and National Educational Television, as well as all of the affiliated stations – each station pays to show our program. It's a unique kind of funding in educational television. With this help, now our program has a budget of $6000. It may sound like quite a difference, but $6000 pays for less than two minutes of cartoons. Two minutes of animated, what I sometimes say, bombardment. I'm very much concerned, as I know you are, about what's being delivered to our children in this country. And I've worked in the field of child development for six years now, trying to understand the inner needs of children. We deal with such things as – as the inner drama of childhood. We don't have to bop somebody over the head to...make drama on the screen. We deal with such things as getting a haircut, or the feelings about brothers and sisters, and the kind of anger that arises in simple family situations. And we speak to it constructively.

Senator Pastore: How long of a program is it?

Mr. Rogers: It's a half hour every day. Most channels schedule it in the noontime as well as in the evening. WETA here has scheduled it in the late afternoon.

Senator Pastore: Could we get a copy of this so that we can see it? Maybe not today, but I›d like to see the program.

Mr. Rogers: I'd like very much for you to see it.

Senator Pastore: I'd like to see the program itself, or any one of them.

Mr. Rogers: We made a hundred programs for EEN, the Eastern Educational Network, and then when the money ran out, people in Boston and Pittsburgh and Chicago all came to the fore and said we›ve got to have more of this neighborhood expression of care. And this is what – this is what I give. I give an expression of care every day to each child, to help him realize that he is unique. I end the program by saying, "You've made this day a special day, by just your being you. There's no person in the whole world like you, and I like you, just the way you are." And I feel that if we in public television can only make it clear that feelings are mentionable and manageable, we will have done a great service for mental health. I think that it's much more dramatic that two men could be working out their feelings of anger – much more dramatic than showing something of gunfire. I'm constantly concerned about what our children are seeing, and for 15 years I have tried in this country and Canada, to present what I feel is a meaningful expression of care.

Senator Pastore: Do you narrate it?

Mr. Rogers: I'm the host, yes. And I do all the puppets and I write all the music, and I write all the scripts –

Senator Pastore: Well, I'm supposed to be a pretty tough guy, and this is the first time I've had goose bumps for the last two days.

Mr. Rogers: Well, I⟩m grateful, not only for your goose bumps, but for your interest in – in our kind of communication. Could I tell you the words of one of the songs, which I feel is very important?

Senator Pastore: Yes.

Mr. Rogers: This has to do with that good feeling of control which I feel that children need to know is there. And it starts out, "What do you do with the mad that you feel?» And that first line came straight from a child. I work with children doing puppets in – in very personal communication with small groups:

> *What do you do with the mad that you feel? When you feel so mad you could bite. When the whole wide world seems oh so wrong, and nothing you do seems very right. What do you do? Do you punch a bag? Do you pound some clay or some dough? Do you round up friends for a game of tag or see how fast you go? It's great to be able to stop when you've planned a thing*

151

that's wrong. And be able to do something else instead, and think this song –

'I can stop when I want to. Can stop when I wish. Can stop, stop, stop anytime… And what a good feeling to feel like this! And know that the feeling is really mine. Know that there's something deep inside that helps us become what we can. For a girl can be someday a lady, and a boy can be someday a man.'

Senator Pastore: I think it›s wonderful. I think it›s wonderful. Looks like you just earned the 20 million dollars.

Read that again. "*I think it's wonderful. Looks like you just earned 20 million dollars.*" Wow. In less than 6 minutes. Want that kind of power? You can have it. Let's analyze how he did that.

First, look at how Senator Pastore addressed Mr. Rogers – he just calls him "Rogers" – no Mr. Slightly disrespectful. Showing him who has more power and trying to intimidate him.

Nonplussed, Mr. Rogers goes forward, respectful and polite, knowing that he is dealing with a personality that is not only difficult but relishes in his reputation for being difficult.

*Senator Pastore, this is a philosophical statement and would take about ten minutes to read, so I'll not do that. One of the first things that a child learns in a healthy family is trust, and **I trust what*** *you have said that you will read this. It's very important to me. I care deeply about children.*

Here, Mr. Rogers used the embedded command when he said, "I *trust what you said that you will read this.*" He also talked about how children learn how to trust and how much he deeply cares about children. What was he saying here? That if you don't read this, Senator Pastore, then you don't believe in happy families, or in the idea that children need to learn how to trust, and you certainly don't care about children.

The response from Senator Pastore? Still gruff. *Will it make you happy if I read it?* What does that sound like to you? He was being patronizing, perhaps argumentative and maybe even a little bit sarcastic. No buy in from Senator Pastore quite yet.

Next, Mr. Rogers ignores the condescending tone and presses forward, acting as if it were the most normal and regular question ever. Let's analyze his response.

*I'd just like to talk about it, **if it's alright**. My first children's program was on WQED fifteen years ago, and its budget was $30. **Now, with the help of the Sears-Roebuck Foundation and National Educational Television, as well as all of the affiliated stations -- each station pays to show our program. It's a unique kind of funding in educational television. With this help, now our program has a budget of $6000. It may sound*** *like quite a difference, but $6000 pays for less than two minutes of cartoons. Two minutes of animated, what I sometimes say, bombardment. I'm very much concerned, as I know you are, about what's being delivered to our children in this country. And I've worked in the field of child development for six years now, trying to understand the inner needs of children. We deal with such things as -- as the inner drama of childhood. We don't have to bop somebody over the head to...make drama on the screen.* We deal with such things as getting a haircut, or the feelings about brothers and sisters, and the kind of anger that arises in simple family situations. And **we speak to it constructively.**

First, he says he'd like to talk about *if it's all right.* He knows that he has the floor, but by asking Senator Pastore if it is all right, he is getting the senator to say that he wants him to speak. By saying it is all right, he is giving his blessing for him to speak. This is a very subtle way for Mr. Rogers to get Sen. Pastore to do what he wants him to do – listen to what he is going to say.

Next, he peppers his request with lots of data. Mr. Rogers has done his research. He knows his internal value and has subtly communicated that to Senator Pastore. Now he is establishing his value in the marketplace as well with providing hard numbers as to how much it costs to produce a show and what the value is, not just to him, but to our community and to our society at large, by investing one of our biggest future assets, our children.

Notice how while he is providing his data and research, he is weaving in his embedded command... "I am very much concerned, **as I know you are**..." He is telling Senator Pastore that he must be concerned with what's being delivered to children on television.

He also says "we don't have to bop somebody over the head..." This is a message to Senator Pastore that he, Mr. Rogers, is not going to bop his message over anyone's head either, because **he can speak to these issues constructively** *(as he is here)*. He is covertly saying to Senator Pastore to listen to his message right here, right now, because he is speaking to a very important issue in a constructive manner.

Watch how Senator Pastore is already starting to soften:

Senator Pastore: *How long of a program is it?*

Oh! I think someone is showing a little interest!

Mr. Rogers: *It's a half hour every day. Most channels schedule it in the noontime hour as well as in the evening. WETA here has scheduled it in the late afternoon.*

Senator Pastore: *Could we get a copy of this so that we can see it? Maybe not today, but I'd like to see the program.*

Notice here – he'd like to see the program. Just a few minutes ago, he didn't even want to read Mr. Rogers' statement. Now he's willing to sit and watch an entire episode of the program.

Mr. Rogers: *'d like very much for you to see it.*

Mr. Rogers is showing that he "sees" Senator Pastore – that he means something – that he has value – all by *how* he responds here. He doesn't say "you should watch it" or "check it out." Instead, he says *I'd very much like* – meaning he would personally be honored for Senator Pastore to watch the program. He is showing Sen. Pastore that how much he respects his opinion.

Senator Pastore: *I'd like to see the program itself, or any one of them.*

Softening. Softening and buying in. Slowly buying in.

Hastening to capitalize on that momentum, Mr. Rogers continues. Also, incidentally, be sure to notice how Mr. Rogers uses a lot of languaging that makes it appear that he and Senator Pastore are in agreement on a lot of areas. He has him agreeing that he will read his statement, that children need to learn how to trust, that happy families are important, that good quality programming for children is important.

*Mr. Rogers: We made a hundred programs for EEN, the Eastern Educational Network, and then when the money ran out, people in Boston and Pittsburgh and Chicago **all came to the fore and said we've got to have more of this neighborhood expression of care.** And this is what – This is what I give. I give an expression of care every day to each child, to help him realize that he is unique. I end the program by saying, "You've made this day a special day, by just your being you. **There's no person in the whole world like you, and I like you, just the way you are.**" And I feel that if we in public television can only make it clear that feelings are mentionable and manageable, we will have done a great service for mental health. **I think that it's much more dramatic that two men could be working out their feelings of anger – much more dramatic than showing something of gunfire.** I'm constantly concerned about what our children are seeing, and for 15 years I have tried in this country and Canada, **to present what I feel is a meaningful expression of care.**

Above, Mr. Rogers jumps right in to continue and show that when his funding ran out before, communities came together in a "neighborly" way and saved the show by donating money. Implicit in what he is saying is that the show brought the community together and also motivated the community to work together. The community also saw such value in the show that they provided grassroots funding for it.

Then he is speaking directly to the inner child, that little vulnerable self that laid deep inside Senator Pastore himself. He said to him that there is no person in the whole world like him and that he, Fred Rogers, liked him just the way he was.

Finally, he embeds the thoughts into Senator Pastore's head that, rather than gunfire or fighting, even grown men are capable of expressing meaningful expressions of care. He is also telling Senator Pastore that he cares about him as a person.

Senator Pastore: *Do you narrate it?*

Now, Senator Pastore is sold on Mr. Rogers. He wants to know if Mr. Rogers is the one who is narrating it, who is hosting it, who is the face of it. He likes Mr. Rogers.

Mr. Rogers: I'm the host, yes. And I do all the puppets and I write all the music, and I write all the scripts –

Mr. Rogers starts to tell him that he is not only the narrator, but the whole show is his creation – everything about it.

Senator Pastore: Well, I'm supposed to be a pretty tough guy, and this is the first time I've had goose bumps for the last two days.

Senator Pastore actually cuts off Mr. Rogers – he is overtaken with emotion that this self-proclaimed "tough guy" actually has goosebumps. Not only does he have the goosebumps, but he interrupts Mr. Rogers to tell him that he has goose bumps! He is overwhelmed.

> **Mr. Rogers:** *Well, I'm grateful, not only for your goose bumps, but for your interest in – in our kind of communication. Could I tell you the words of one of the songs, which I feel is very important?*

Mr. Rogers is very savvy here. He hears that Senator Pastore has goosebumps but he instinctively knows that he isn't to the finish line yet. He is very close but knows he needs to get there to win the prize. So he embeds another command when he says that he is grateful for his goosebumps (remember this a way to build rapport – mirror back what the person has said to you) but he is also grateful "*for your interest in our kind of communication.*" Now, Senator Pastore didn't really say that, now did he? But he was buying into what Mr. Rogers was selling so Mr. Rogers told him what to think when he said that he was grateful for his "interest" in his way of communicating.

> **Senator Pastore:** *Yes.*

He is eating out of Mr. Rogers' hand now. He will say yes to anything Mr. Rogers asks at this point.

Mr. Rogers: This has to do with that good feeling of control which I feel that children need to know is there. And it starts out, «What do you do with the mad that you feel?» And that first line came straight from a child. I work with children doing puppets in – in very personal communication with small groups.

He goes on to tell him the words of a song. A song that shows how he sees the meaning and value in children as human beings.

Finally, you can almost feel the rough, gruff, and tough Senator Pastore nearly wiping away tears as he exclaims:

Senator Pastore: I think it's wonderful. I think it's wonderful. Looks like you just earned the 20 million dollars.

He actually repeats how wonderful it is! He is feeling elated and ready to do the Snoopy happy dance – and remember that he is the one who approved the funding! He wasn't *receiving* this money. He was approving the dollars for it, and yet he was thrilled and moved to emotion!

The Mr. Rogers example is a perfect one. He could have believed he had no chance. He could have said that Senator Pastore was way more powerful than he was. He could have said that Senator Pastore was super difficult. He could have not even bothered to try because of the uphill climb. Remember at that time, Mr. Rogers' show had only been on the air for one year. He wasn't the legend that we know him to be today. He was some guy from Pittsburgh with a fledgling show that he believed in. That is all. Because he took a chance, and provided a compelling argument, utilizing many of the tools provided to you in this book, he won millions of dollars for his show, and the rest became history!

Here are couple of other tips that Mr. Rogers' employed while persuading Senator Pastore to give him $20 Million:

1. *Be firm in your request but not demanding.*

    Notice how Mr. Rogers wasn't asking in a manner that was demanding. He didn't say "Give me the money" and he wasn't obnoxious. He didn't say "If you don't give me the money, then obviously you don't care about kids. The whole country will know that our legislature doesn't care about children. Is that what you want?" Taking a tone that is belligerent or tries to guilt the other person into doing what you want, will often have the opposite effect. This is true in general, but it is especially true if you have a difficult personality on the other side. A difficult personality is usually a person who is a control freak and control freaks will resist any sort of overt manipulation.

    You want to appear that you are being inviting, so that the person believes that you are having a pleasant conversation with him or her. The other person knows that you are asking for something, and you want to have ears that are listening, not ears that have been shut down because now they have become defensive.

2. *Exude confidence, not desperation.*

Notice how Mr. Rogers quietly was telling Senator Pastore what it was that he wanted and then layered in his data and embedded commands along the way. At no time did he sound desperate or needy.

Years ago, when I worked for a bank, the lenders had an inside joke that went something like "we only lend money to people who don't actually need it." While it was sort of joke, it was sort of true in a way.

Psychologically, we humans are quirky in this way. We often want to be friends with people who don't need us, and we only want to give to charities that are already solvent. We want to know that there is value in what we are investing our time. If someone appears needy or desperate then we instinctively feel as though there is no value there.

This means that when making requests, you have to find that delicate balance between asking for what you want, and doing it in such a way that feels inviting, as if you are being asked to dine at a fine restaurant. If you are making your request in a way that sounds as if you are begging, then your confidence level is not there, and most importantly, your feeling of that inherent internal value is lacking. You want the other side to know that you matter so you must demonstrate to them that you have value.

So when you are embedding commands and having your dialogue with the other side, it is imperative that you are confident, not cocky and firm, and not demanding. Demanding will not get you what you want. Forceful is not what you want to be. You don't want to – as Mr. Rogers said – bop anyone over the head. You want to draw them in, as if you are the magnet and they are the steel (cue the old song). You want to your words to be compelling because they come from a place of a knowing inner value and feeling secure in that.

The more you push – the more the other side will feel the need to push back. When you do resistance exercises, you push and you feel that push right back. That is what happens when you are trying to pressure someone into doing something and they feel that pressure. Most people will not respond positively to that kind of approach.

In other words, you want the other person not only to do what you want them to do, but you want them to **want** to do it.

How do you lead them to a decision? Just the way Mr. Rogers did in the example above. You want to inspire not tire. You can definitely choose the alternative and be menacing and threatening and beat someone down until they relent and give in to your demands. But what will happen after that is they will regret having given in most of the time. Then they will be back and will make your life miserable!

In law, they will file appeals or actions for modification. In the rest of the world, they may bad-mouth you, quit, turn other employees against you, turn other potential buyers of your product away and the list goes on.

How to ask a person for the meeting?

When you go to ask the person for the negotiation meeting, in addition to finding the right time to ask them as we discussed in the foregoing, you will want to come across as confident, respectful and not demanding. Obviously, the words you will use will differ slightly depending upon each situation but here are a few examples:

Jim, I'd like to discuss my future with the firm with you and the value that I think that I can continue to bring. I have some ideas. Send me some dates and times that you are available in the next week or two, and I will be sure to make myself available so that we can get something scheduled.

Here you might want to discuss a raise, a promotion or more benefits to you – but you frame it in a way that you are going to be giving additional benefit to the company too. The additional benefit may only be that you will continue to perform in the way that you have in the past. When you get into that meeting, be ready to provide concrete facts and data as to how you have provided value to the company in the past and how you will continue to do so in the future. Don't be afraid to toot your own horn but do it in a way that doesn't sound boastful but rather, sounds matter of fact, firm and confident.

Be careful not to sound desperate or even worse, entitled.

Jim, I need to talk you about increasing my compensation. I can't live on what I'm making.

As an employer myself, I know that an approach like that would immediately put me on the defensive. It would make me think that the person is trying to make me feel as if I hadn't been paying that person enough and that I should feel guilty or ashamed. Since I wouldn't likely feel either, I would just be annoyed that I have to defend myself and not feel very gratuitous.

Putting the latter exchange in terms of the You Matter paradigm – the message to the employer is "you don't see that I matter because you haven't been paying me enough." The employer's feeling would then be "well you don't see that *I* matter because you haven't appreciated all I've done for you as an employer." This means that the conversation begins with both parties in a bit of a huff, nursing their, "I don't matter enough to you" wounds. This is not the setup for a winning negotiation.

The first script has both parties in the same place ultimately – sitting down to discuss what the person wants. But in the first approach, the employer feels respected and valued, and thus ready to do what you want.

How to Ask for What You Want

This is where the rubber hits the road and where the fear starts to sink in. I once did a meditation class where the teacher asked us to visualize what we feared the most. He then asked us to keep our eyes closed and create a physical manifestation of what that fear looked like. He said it could be anything we wanted it to be. For me, the vision of black hole came into my mind. So there I was standing in the room, my eyes closed, envisioning a huge black hole in front of me. The teacher then asked us to step toward that physical manifestation of the fear. I suddenly felt this grip in my chest because if I stepped forward, I would step into that black hole and then what would happen? I would disappear? Pain of some kind would ensue? I really didn't know. But here's the crazy thing that happened next in my vision. I stepped forward into that black hole and once I got there, it came to me that it was just an illusion of a black hole. It looked black from my point of view from where I was standing, but once I got into it, I realized it was just a shallow indentation in the land. It was maybe only an inch or two deep and not scary at all. What a revelation that was for me! All fear is that way.

Remember that FEAR is actually an acronym for **F**alse **E**vidence **A**ppearing **R**eal. It really is the biggest time waster, along with worrying and complaining. We seem to think, as humans, that engaging in these activities somehow helps us. That perhaps maybe we can control outcomes in this way. This is truly the biggest scam in history. You cannot speak words of what you don't want to happen over and over and over again and expect the universe to bring you the opposite of that. It just doesn't work that way.

Instead visualize how you want things to go. Even if you have had a bad day. You had an exchange with someone that didn't go the way you planned it. That night, your exercise is to replay the day, including that poor exchange and rewrite it either in your head or on paper, and change the dialog and events so it looks like the way it would have gone had you scripted it. Remember like attracts like (another law of physics) and your thoughts are energy so be sure that you are having the thoughts you want to have so they attract the things into your life that you want to attract.

So with all of that as your prefatory into this next part of the conversation, let's discuss how you ask for what you want.

You will start with areas of agreement, as we discussed above, as well as acknowledging the value and meaning that either the person you are speaking to or their company has for you, then go into what it is that you want and what your value is that shows why you should have it. Here is an example:

Jim, I am grateful and thrilled to be part of this team. I especially appreciate the integrity this company has and the care that each member of our team has for the clients and for each other internally. I am also proud to be part of an organization that is so knowledgeable and delivers quality products and services to the clients. For my part, it has been great to be able to achieve _____ goals. I am proud that I have exceeded my goals by ___ % and that I have brought on ___ number of new clients. Recently I had a conversation with Joe Client and he really appreciated that I _____ (whatever you might have done for a client that was above and beyond, or that the client really appreciated). I enjoy contributing to this company's success. I have done the research and other companies of this size in this industry pay _____ (whatever your position is) this amount on average _____ (state the range). I am currently at _____ (state your salary) which represents the lower end of the range. I am therefore requesting _____ (a raise, benefits, whatever) and I believe that I am worth that based upon what I have contributed to this company and what the current ranges are for others in my position. I very much appreciate your consideration, and look forward to contributing to the continued growth of this company.

Obviously, you can change this to conform to your situation. Perhaps it isn't hard numbers you've contributed but that you're the one that they call upon to deal with the difficult clients all the time or who calls the service people and deals with copier when it jams. As an employer myself, I know the non-monetary value of employees who save me headaches and allow me to be more efficient in other areas.

Don't Apologize (or Even Sound Apologetic)

You can see that in the above exchange, you are not apologizing. As soon as you start apologizing, you are sending a message that you don't matter as much. Remember, you want to communicate that you have value, that you mean something, that you MATTER! Starting off a sentence with "sorry" is like saying you're the Blue Light Special at K-Mart or the clearance rack at Sears. The other side might take a look because they are looking for a bargain, but they will assume that they will be able to take it or leave it.

I once had an attorney who was working for me who was brilliant, but he lacked self-confidence. In the spirit of teaching him the mechanics of how to put together a winning family law trial, I worked with him on a huge custody trial, teaching him everything step by step. Together, we prepared the opening statement, the closing argument, the direct examinations, the cross examinations and all the exhibit notebooks. We discussed the strategy of the case, the tactics of the case, and everything in between. I even sat there during the trial and participated by doing parts of it with him. He was 100% ready for that trial. Now, just as in negotiations, you can't script everything in a trial, but you can anticipate what the other side is going to argue and be prepared to refute that.

During the trial, we get to a part where we are going to introduce some text messages between the husband and the wife as an exhibit. These types of correspondence are definitely hearsay under the rules of evidence and so in order to have the court accept them as official pieces of evidence which the judge can look at and consider in making his or her ruling, they have to fall into an "exception" to the hearsay rule. Immediately, we got an objection from the opposing attorney.

"Objection! Hearsay!" the opposing attorney shouts out with resolve. She then launches into the rule and why it doesn't even fall into an exception. Technical stuff that I won't bore you with here.

My associate attorney then says in a very apologetic and sheepish way, *"Its, um, uh, an exception, because (clears throat) the parties who wrote it, are here and, uh, can, um state, er um, I mean testify to, it's um, reliability, I mean, they can, uh, testify that the contents, are, um correct, or I mean, accurate, yes that they are accurate representations."*

Painful, right? So the judge decides to hold off on ruling and allows the attorney to lay what we call a "predicate", which means she was going to allow the attorney to ask the questions that needed to be asked to lay a "foundation" that the texts were written by our client and that they were a true and accurate representation of what had been written. He does that, then again offers the texts into evidence but says it like this:

"So, now, I (shoulder shrug) guess I offer this into evidence (purses lips showing that he knows the judge isn't going to allow it)."

Up jumps opposing counsel, who shouts, *"I renew my objection on the same grounds!"* No apologetic tone there.

So guess what happened? That's exactly right.

"Objection SUSTAINED!" declared the judge matter-of-factly.

The attorney basically told the judge what to rule. We had even gone over it beforehand, and he knew what arguments to make. Those texts were clearly an exception to the hearsay rule and had he presented it with confidence and with the statute and caselaw to back it up in a way that was firm but respectful, he would have prevailed on that issue.

Along with the word "sorry", here are a few other words and phrases that have no place in your negotiation conversation:

I'll take it! (to the very first offer)

I need the money/can't afford (and the like)

What I need to live on is _____

Everyone I have spoken to has said _____

I know that Mary makes more/less than I do, so I should make _____

I want at least _____ (x amount). (If you say this, this is what you will get)

No. (You can say that you aren't accepting an offer but put it in terms that the other person feels heard.)

Remember the key is to prove your own value, while preserving the other person's feeling of his or hers. The above phrases either devalue yourself, don't have anything to do with your value, or don't give the other person a reason that you have value to them.

As my father used to say – whatever you say, say it with authority, and people will believe you.

Leave Winging It to the Birds

While we can't actually script anything in the courtroom or anything with regard to negotiation, you also don't have to be in a position where you are making things up as you go along. Do not wing it. Especially if it is something that is really important to you and you want a favorable outcome. You will want to approach it with a certain discipline in your preparation and a certain mindset. Once you are in there then you will be ready to go with the flow to a certain extent. You will be able to improvise when you need to but in a very controlled and expected way. It may sound counterintuitive but the more prepared you are, the more ready you will be to improvise and be flexible.

Just look at the best jazz or rock musicians in the world. They can riff off and play all sort of versions of songs and it all sounds like it makes sense. My mother is actually a super talented pianist and can play "Happy Birthday" so that it sounds like Beethoven, or so that it sounds like a country music song, but she didn't just sit down at the piano and do that. She had to be a master first.

Once you become a master negotiator, you will know that you still need to do the work of preparation and then you will be ready for any sort of improvisation that you need to do while you are in the thick of it.

It's Not Fair!!

I recently heard the best quote. *Fair is for the Ferris Wheel at the fair!* A great line. It totally sums up my thoughts about what the word "fair" means.

I have been interviewed on the national television program *Extra* a number of times. Once, I was commentating on the Brad and Angelina divorce but while I was being interviewed, they asked me about another celebrity couple who had started off saying they were going to settle their case behind closed doors in negotiations but now it appeared that the communications had broken down. The interviewer asked me to comment on why I thought that had happened. I responded the way I always do when I am asked about situations such as these.

Every single person who has walked into my divorce attorney offices has said to me that they don't want to fight. They want an amicable divorce. They don't want to spend a lot of money on attorneys' fees. BUT and this is a big but – they also want what's "FAIR".

So what's the problem? The problem is that every single person has a different idea about what FAIR means. This is what I really think it means in negotiation:

Fantasy Agreement In your Reality

A lot goes into what we think is "fair". Our version of fair has to do only with our perceptions of what we think our value is, what we think the other person's value is, what we think justice requires. There is the intellectual version of what is "fair" and then there is the emotional version of what is "fair." Both are playing ball on a regular basis inside our heads and sometimes the outside world is in harmony with our inner dialog and many times it is not.

As a divorce attorney, I often have a talk with my clients that applies to everything in life. I call it the divorce law versus divorce justice conversation. There is divorce law – which is what will be applied in a case. Divorce law definitely has a range of possibilities and within that land is where one can expect to fall, should a case not settle through negotiations outside of court and the parties land in front of a judge. A judge does not have the power to make his or her own choices outside the law. They are tasked to apply the law.

Then there is divorce "justice". This has nothing to do with the law. This is what the party wants because they think the other side should be punished for their bad behavior. Examples of bad behavior might be cheating, breaking up the family, shaming the other party, causing the case to be over-litigated unnecessarily, accusing them of doing things that they didn't, abusing them, being an addict, spending money they didn't think should have been spent, and the list is actually endless but you get the point.

While a judge has the authority to consider some of those things, consideration can only be whatever consideration a statute gives the judge to permission to look into.

Time and time again I have heard clients say, "how can he or she get away with this!??" I have to remind them that first, the only person who has any power over anyone in the court system is the judge and second, that the judge has power only to the extent that the law provides that power. Nothing more.

In the rest of the world of negotiations, the feelings are the same. Going back to my example of the paralegal who felt that if she were valued and appreciated, she would basically have been paid the same as the partners and would have been able to take off the same amount of time. I remind you to have infinite feelings of internal power and value, but to be aware of what your value is in the external world. And don't collapse your emotions into areas that have objective criteria.

Forget Fairness and Focus on Facts and Issues
The way to combat the "fairness" conversation and be sure to stay on track is to stay within the lanes of the issues, facts and data. Stay away from focusing on the people or the back stories or what you "think" might be going on. All of that sort of thing just keeps you from being present to a solution to the actual issues at hand.

How Men and Women Negotiate Differently

In Chapter 6, we touched upon a few of the ways that men and women negotiate differently. There are several others. Bear in mind, none of the traits are right or wrong, and there is never an absolute with regard to a gender, or a human being for that matter. These are just few general guidelines that might be helpful when preparing for that big day.

As I mentioned earlier, men have a much greater ability to compartmentalize things. This is not to say that they are not impacted by things emotionally. They certainly are and sometimes to their detriment as our society, while better, still compels men to keep that "stiff upper lip" to the extent possible. But in negotiations they more easily are able to put aside other things that are going on in their minds and just think about the task at hand.

Women, on the other hand, have a different sort of brain. The brain is actually much more connected to the emotions section of the brain. Because a women's thinking brain has a direct connection to her emotional brain, she is much more likely to sit in a negotiation and wonder if the other side likes her, if she is being judged, and then can actually be hurt or take things more personally.

In my divorce mediations, women would sit in front of their soon to be ex-husbands and expect him to see the person who gave up her life for them, bore their children, helped them through school, and well, you get the picture. Men, conversely,

176

don't see any of that during those mediations. They see a business transaction. That puts men at a bit of an advantage because they are able to keep their emotions more in check. In business mediations, the feelings and interactions might be similar even without the personal relationship component.

There is another way that gender plays a role in negotiations. We definitely know that women are less apt to try to negotiate anything at all. Men aren't running to negotiate either.

In one Harvard study on which gender was more likely to *initiate* negotiations, the results were very enlightening. In this study, both men and women were asked to initiate a conversation with their employer to ask for additional compensation. What they found was:

- Men were significantly more likely to start a negotiation for more pay. On average, 42% of male students began a conversation to negotiate for more compensation, whereas only 28% of female students initiated a negotiation on that issue.
- Men were two times as likely as women to begin a conversation to negotiate if their counterpart was *female* – 46% of male students, but only 23% of female students asked for higher compensation when facing a female counterpart.
- On the contrary, there was no significant difference between men and women in the propensity to initiate

a compensation negotiation when their counterpart was *male.*

In reviewing the results, it appears that men are less intimidated if the counterpart is going to be female than they are if the counterpart is going to be a male. Neither side felt particularly more or less intimidated by negotiating with a male. That may be because of perceptions. Perceptions that women are more difficult, that women are less apt to bend the rules, or perceptions that women are more emotional.

There is also a perception that women take risks differently. The generally accepted idea is that men are more apt to take risks and women much less so. Women are perceived as being more risk averse but in reality, they actually just take more time to make decisions, because their decisions are driven more by emotion. I say that with caution. When I say that, it can conjure the image of a hysterical woman who is out of emotional control. Even the word "hysterical" rubs me, as a woman who has been in a position of power for a long time, the wrong way. It sounds misogynistic. What I mean is that women want to feel, intuitively, that they are making the right choice. Whereas men, perhaps because they trust their decision-making choices more readily, are much more apt to jump right into the pool.

Years ago, when I was in wealth management, we developed business by doing seminars. (It might still be that way.) What I found was that men could show up at some local high-end steak restaurant, listen to one presentation on capital markets or some such general topic, and make a snap decision to switch brokerage houses. Women, on the other hand, would rarely make such a snap choice. I found that I had to have a series of seminars or events. So I started something I called "The Empowered Women Series" and there were five sessions in the series that I would run for five weeks in a row. The first week was a life coach or something motivational, the second week was me presenting on the basics of finance, the third week was a physician discussing something related to women's health issues, and so forth. Because each topic/speaker was such a draw so they would always sell out, I created a rule that each woman HAD to sign up for all five sessions, otherwise they would be placed on a waitlist.

My rule that they had to come to all five sessions was very strategic. I knew that women don't generally make decisions quickly. They want to get to know a person before they would even consider moving their money. Even if they don't love their current wealth managers, they might feel loyal, or they prefer the "devil they know", or maybe their late husband chose that person, so they feel that person has already been "vetted". After each session, I would call each woman and thank them for coming. I said nothing about moving their money, or meeting with me, and didn't ask how satisfied they were with current advisors. Nothing. That is, until after the last session. Only then would I call again, and then listen to them gush about how wonderful the series was, how many friends they made, and how much they learned. It was at that point that I would then say something like, "I'm so grateful that I have been able to provide so much value to you. I'd love to invite you in to have lunch here with me now so that we can talk about ways that I can continue to do that."

I showed them value. I showed them that they meant something to me. There was never a hard sell. No one wants the hard sell. Both men and women disdain the feeling that someone is pushing something on them. It feels desperate, which remember, sends the discount signal.

Both (all) genders have risks associated with how they negotiate. The risks all come back to whether or not the deal will hold together. You want a deal that is going to stick. The only deals that tend to stick together for the long term are the ones where both sides walk away feeling as if they matter, and that they feel got something which satisfies their need to feel valuable.

Obviously, a generalization but men should be aware of these traps:

- Pushing a deal when the other person doesn't really want it.
- Appearing controlling
- Rushing a deal (either for the other person or jumping into it themselves)

- Getting angry with feelings of vengeance

Women should be stay clear of:

- Getting emotional (crying, anger, feelings of vengeance)
  Being too careful and too slow to decide (the other side might change their mind about an offer on the table while you're taking your time)
  Allowing yourself to be pushed into a decision because you don't want to look bad, because you feel you're asking for too much, or because you just want it over.

Both (all) genders should be wary of:

> Making decisions out of guilt, resentment, fear, anger or feeling defeated or resigned. (Negotiating from these places will cause agreements that one will eventually regret.)
> Negotiating too early (not having done the proper preparation)

Women and men are absolutely equally capable of negotiating at the highest level and both are excellent at persuading people. Neither gender has any sort of edge when you understand the differences. Both genders (and all in between) arrive at the same place when negotiation is done right. The difference really is in how each arrives at that place.

Visualize Your Outcome

You're almost ready to walk in and have that conversation. You have done the internal work, you have done your research, created your arguments, figured out your leverage, created your first offer, determined what you will wear and you have practiced the body language skills. Now it is time to picture how the conversation is going to go. At that end of this chapter will be a visualization exercise. I strongly recommend you take the time to picture it. Picture yourself in the position of winning. What will that be like? How will your life change? Live in that future as if it is now.

EXERCISES

1. What are the areas that potentially are emotional for me in this negotiation?

   _____

   _____

   _____

   _____

   _____

   _____

2. If I am triggered, what types of emotions am I going to likely feel?

   _____

   _____

   _____

   _____

   _____

3. What are examples of some things that the other person could say or do that might trigger my emotions?

   _____

   _____

   _____

   _____

   _____

4. Do I feel that there is an imbalance of power in this upcoming negotiation? Why do I feel that way? And then what will I do about that?

_____

_____

_____

_____

_____

_____

5. Do I believe that the other side is overly difficult, narcissistic or just incorrigible? If so, why?

_____

_____

_____

_____

_____

_____

6. Write out exactly what to say.

_____

_____

_____

_____

_____

7. Now reframe the above in the form of embedded commands.

_____

_____

_____

_____

_____

_____

8. How will I ask the person for a meeting? (Exact script!)

_____

_____

_____

_____

_____

9. How will I ask for what I want?

_____

_____

_____

_____

_____

BEFORE NEGOTIATING, VISUALIZE

10. Before that meeting, or that conversation, visualize your outcomes. Don't just visualize what you want from the outcome. Also visualize how it is going to go. Work through

the conversations and what people are going to say to each other. Also remember:

- Stay away from any visions, thoughts or people who will detract you from your creation.
- Set boundaries for personal and professional value.
- Ask yourself – Who are you for yourself?
- Also ask – Who do you visualize yourself to be?
- Picture the other person and how they are going to respond to you.

11. Write out your scripts detailing what you want to say.

_____

_____

_____

_____

_____

_____

12. Now take what you wrote above and try to reframe it in the form of an embedded command.

_____

_____

_____

_____

_____

13. Does that sound more persuasive?

_____

_____

_____

_____

_____

_____

Either close your eyes or write out this exercise.

Picture the other person sitting in the room as you enter. What is that person wearing? What does that person look like exactly?

_____

_____

_____

_____

_____

How are you walking in? What are you wearing?

_____

_____

_____

_____

_____

What does the other person say?

_____

_____

_____

_____

_____

Will you shake his or her hand? How will you shake the hand? Will you make eye contact?

_____

_____

_____

_____

What will you say first?

_____

_____

_____

_____

How will you say it?

_____

_____

_____

_____

_____

_____

How does the other person respond?

_____

_____

_____

_____

What will the conversation look like after you've walked in?

_____

_____

_____

_____

Who is leading the discussion?

_____

_____

_____

_____

What is the final result of the conversation?

_____

_____

_____

_____

_____

_____

Chapter 7 – "R" – Record All Agreements in Writing

"If you didn't get it in writing, it never happened."
~Your Litigation Attorney When You Try to Sue on A Verbal
Agreement

TAKEAWAYS FROM THIS CHAPTER:

- Record any and all agreements in some form of writing. It reduces the risk of misunderstandings and will make your life easier down the road
- Even if you didn't resolve your issues in your negotiation, you can learn a lot from every interaction with the other person and then use that information for the next time you want to persuade them to do something you want them to do, or use what you learned in a subsequent negotiation

Get It in Writing, Any Kind of Writing

Here, you want to make sure that even if you come to an informal agreement about something with your teenager, if it is important enough, you will want to make sure you memorialize it in some sort of writing. It could be a text message, an email or a handwritten note. It doesn't have to (necessarily) be signed in the presence of two witnesses, notarized and signed in blood. You want to reduce the possibility of potential misunderstandings down the road.

In law, there is something called parol (yes, it is parol not parole – this has nothing to do with prison) evidence. This is usually not allowed when trying to prove the terms of a contract. The contract is supposed to speak for itself and parol evidence is any kind of information that one of the parties to the contract tries to present to the judge to prove that there were some other terms to the contract. These would be terms that aren't in the writing. An example of this might be that a painter agrees to paint a person's house. In exchange, the homeowner is going to pay the painter a sum of money. They memorialize that into a written agreement. Then later, a dispute arises, and the painter and the homeowner end up before a judge slinging arrows at each other. The dispute is around terms that were not directly addressed in the contract. The painter says that the homeowner agreed to pay for all the materials separately – that the contract was for labor only. The homeowner says that there was no other discussion other than what ultimately ended up in the contract. The painter then wants to present witnesses or other evidence to prove that there were additional terms to the contract. In court the painter will generally not be able to do that. The painter might be able to try to prove that the contract meant labor only. But the courts generally will not allow either side to prove that there were additional terms.

Most formal contracts have something called a merger clause and an integration clause. These clauses both serve the same purpose in that they state that there are no other agreements between the parties. They stand for the idea that the writing that the parties are signing represents their full and final agreement and that there are no side or oral agreements or other contingencies that would change the meaning or effect of the contract.

In the real world, you can still protect yourself with a follow up writing. It can say something like "I look forward to _____ (the event, working with you)." Or it may say something like, "*Thank you for meeting with me. To confirm, here's what we discussed (then list the points one by one) and here's a summary of what we agreed upon (list the points one by one)*." The key here is to write this confirmation and send it out on a timely basis and also to be specific.

By doing this, you reduce the possibilities of misunder-standings down the road, and if there are differences in what you recollect, they can be handled immediately. In order to handle them right away, the follow up correspondence obviously also must be sent immediately after the conversation. Don't wait a month and a half before sending it. Send it that day or at the longest, the next morning. If you don't receive a

193

response, then you may be able to safely assume that you are on the same page. You might want to simply ask the person to reply, however. In that instance, you would say something like "*Please reply with the word 'agreed' if this accurately summarizes our conversation and agreements.*" But even if you don't ask for or get that confirmation, if you send a written follow up and get no response, then you'll at least have ammunition if there's a disagreement down the road. The conversation would then go "*Well I sent you the written follow up and you didn't respond, so I thought we were on the same page.*"

This doesn't always work mind you. It is just a safeguard, a risk reducer if you will. Years ago, I had accepted a position with a law firm. The partners from that firm didn't send me a formal contract or offer (which is something that, once I owned my own firm, I made a definite practice of doing) so I went ahead and sent them a thank you/acceptance letter, outlining all the terms that I understood to be part of our agreement. Of course, I included the salary, but I also included the benefits and my start date. I understood the benefits to include paying dues on my behalf for the state bar, as well as the local bar and other related organizations. They also had agreed to pay for my health insurance and some limited amount of marketing. The managing partner acknowledged receipt of my correspondence and added that she was very much looking forward to my joining their team.

It all started off as planned. I showed up on the day we had agreed upon and my first paycheck reflected the pay which we had agreed upon. At some point, a few weeks into working at that firm, I asked what the procedure was for having my bar dues paid. I was expecting to hear something like that I would submit an invoice and that they would either pay them directly or reimburse me. That is how it had been done at the previous law firm for which I had worked. I also knew the firms for which my husband had worked had similar types of benefits and processes. He is also a lawyer. Plus, I knew that not only did we have an agreement, but that I had written the confirmation letter and had even received acknowledgment of it. Well, imagine my surprise when they said that they weren't going to pay the dues. Of course, I whipped out that letter like I was drawing a gun from my holster in the Wild West. The managing partner's incredulous response? *"Well, you may have written that, but that's not what it's going to be."*

No shock that I didn't stay too long at that firm! What was really going on there? First, I had negotiated a deal with the firm. I believed the deal we had settled on reflected that they saw my value and they felt that they were getting my skills as an attorney as value to them. Both sides are feeling they have been seen and that they mattered to the other side. I had actually turned down other offers and the partners at this firm knew that, and they had come up to the salary point that I had requested.

Then, at some point, without telling me, they decided to change their agreement. By their not keeping their word, I now felt that they had lost their integrity and more seriously, now I felt taken advantage of. When someone says that they feel the other person is "taking advantage of me," what they are really saying is that "I am not feeling valued and respected." In other words, "I am not feeling I matter." If you don't feel enough value in yourself internally, then when something like the above scenario takes place, you might just let it go. You might say to yourself that you don't really like that they didn't keep their word on the bar dues promise, but all in all it is a good job and so you decide to let it go.

For me, I no longer felt valued. I have worked very hard to be a person of my word and keep my promises not just to others but to myself also. So, when they backed off on this part of their agreement, I became skeptical. I began to wonder what else they weren't going to keep their word on. I began to think maybe they didn't have integrity in the way they conducted themselves in business and with the firm. Just that small thing gave me pause.

When we as humans start to feel doubt about others, then we start to look for things to bolster our doubts and beliefs. Research shows that we humans need five positive things to make up for one negative thing. In other words, unfortunately for us, we are hard wired to focus on the negative. That's why when we do something and everyone in the room says you were phenomenal and one person says you stunk to high heaven and you should go back to hiding under the rock from whence you came, you want to hightail it back to that rock.

The spiral started happening for me after that. I started noticing all sorts of other things that I didn't like about working at that firm. Because of that, more things I didn't like started showing up in my space. I only ended up working for that firm for about 18 months. All because they didn't keep their word and I didn't feel as if they valued me.

No Resolution is Not a Loss

Even if you come away from your negotiation session without having reached your goals or even without any resolutions whatsoever, you will have gained. Every time you have one of these conversations, you learn something about what is incentivizing the other side, what their positions are and what their arguments are. Now you have some homework to do. You know what to prepare for when you have the next meeting with that person, or what to do so that when you do have that next meeting (or are in a similar situation), you have all your ducks in a row.

Remember that your mindset and your attitude are almost everything. While you have control over a lot of the process, you can't control the other person. Some people appear to be out of touch with reality, are beyond difficult or delight in power. You could give up at that point and say they always win. But as one of my best friends always says, "Do you want to be right about that? Or do you want things to change?" You can always turn things around and there is always a way to get your way. Remember that the other side will have his or her way that they see the world. Be aware of that not to slow you down, but so that you can understand it. Meeting with the other person will help you to understand how they think, so that you can strategize better and put together a winning tactical plan. You will learn how to evoke the most constructive behavior from them. You'll know if going forward, you have to offer more of a carrot as an incentive, or alternatively, create more leverage so that they get that incentive they need to sway your direction.

Negotiation provides feedback. If you don't come to an agreement, there are a variety of possible lessons that you could draw. You may conclude that there was no room for agreement, but it may also be possible that you overplayed your hand or weren't sufficiently creative. In other words, you can learn more about your own negotiation strengths and weaknesses.

Be ready to be reflective. When the negotiation is over, ask yourself, "What surprised me? Where could I have been more prepared? What did I discover that I did not foresee? What do I think is motivating them now that I didn't realize before?" While some surprises come out of the blue, in retrospect you might spot certain things that could've been expected and prepared for. You want to look at the process by which you planned for negotiation to sharpen your sense of anticipation in the future.

More than anything, you will have used all the tools you have learned and become not only a skilled negotiator, but a stronger person overall. Each time you face someone who has intimidated you and did it with moxie, you will feel stronger, more self-assured and more powerful.

EXERCISES

1. Think about what agreements you have made with people recently that you need to follow up with in writing. This includes a conversation you might have had with your utilities company, with your spouse, your boss or your neighbor. Write down here which ones need to be confirmed in writing and when you are going to confirm it.

---

2. Now take the people above and practice writing out what you are going to say to them.

---

3. What did I learn about the other person in this negotiation?

_____

_____

_____

_____

_____

_____

_____

_____

4. What surprised me?

_____

_____

_____

_____

_____

_____

_____

5. In what areas could I have been more prepared?

_____

_____

_____

_____

_____

_____

_____

_____

6. What did I learn about myself in this negotiation? What are my strengths and what are my weaknesses?

_____

_____

_____

_____

_____

_____

_____

_____

FINAL THOUGHTS

The Oak Tree

By taking this process from the inside out, you will find that when you are actually negotiating, you will be more like an oak tree; firm, stable and basically unaffected by the wind. Wind may bend an oak tree but when that happens, it just shows its flexibility. Through its leaves, it provides clean air so those who interact with it, receive value. It knows its own intrinsic value. It is totally unaffected by insults, eyerolls, facial expressions and voice tones.

You, the real you, are like that oak tree. You are inherently valuable and you matter. Once you feel that internal value and are unaffected by external factors, you will come from that place of power. If you are trying to derive your internal value from anything external, you always will come up short.

Work Your Way Out

Once you feel your internal value, then start gathering the external information you will need to build your case. Methodically determine what research you need to do, who you need to talk to, what information will be helpful to you and then weave that all together to create the cloak of power that you will wear while having your negotiation conversation.

Impact

The day of the negotiation, be prepared to have impact. No words, body language, or gesture will be wasted. It all will be deliberate. You cannot control the other person but you can control everything about yourself. Be prepared!

Final Words

Remember watching the movie *The Wizard of Oz* as a child? As an adult, I have come to realize all of the meaning in every single part of that movie. Dorothy represents the naïve child in all of us. She experiences a terrible storm, which is representative of the storms we all have to deal with in life. The Scarecrow, Tin Man, and Lion are all parts of ourselves that we universally experience – we sometimes believe we don't have enough brains, that we have to find our heart to feel love in our lives, or feel afraid or cowardly. The Wicked Witch is a symbol of our own worst fears, or our negative inner self-talk manifesting itself. The fab foursome embarked on a journey to find a "wizard" – a mythical and magical figure who was supposedly going to solve all of their problems. This is demonstrative of how we all look outside ourselves to try to satisfy those internal needs.

By facing her fears, Dorothy was able to give the Scarecrow his brain, the Tin Man his heart and the Lion got that courage that he believed he so needed. Then very dramatically, Dorothy poured water right onto the Wicked Witch and made her disappear. She faced her darkest fears and they disappeared.

The huge moment, and my favorite part, was at the point when Dorothy realized everyone else got what they wanted, but she hadn't gotten her wish to go home. She then saw Glinda, the Good Witch, rushed over to her, and implored her to help her. This is perfect analogy of how we all reach a point of desperation, where we want to find ourselves, feel that we have purpose, and know we are valuable.

Glinda then told Dorothy, *"You've always had the power, my dear. You just had to learn it for yourself."*

You have that power.

Now it's time to get out there and negotiate like you MATTER, because you do.

205

NEXT STEPS

Knowledge without application is just information. Changing your habits, your thoughts, your dialog, and the way you interact in the world takes affirmative action. It can be so hard sometimes to make even the smallest of changes in your life, let alone big ones. The task can seem too daunting. So where should you begin?

To get you started, I've created the Winning Negotiation Cheat Sheet. This is your 6 point (M.A.T.T.E.R.) checklist that you can print out and keep in a place where, at a quick glance, you can affirm the new self you are creating yourself to be.

Negotiate Your Best Life.

Become unstoppable: Negotiate with courage and confidence to drive the outcome you want.

Stop what you are doing and head to:
www.WinMyNegotiation.com

and grab your free Winning Negotiation Cheat Sheet.

Today is a great day to start living your dreams.

Printed in the USA
CPSIA information can be obtained
at www.ICGtesting.com
LVHW010452140124
768651LV00012B/734